A
Century
of
Sunderland Cinemas

by

Albert Anderson

Black Cat Publications

ISBN 1 899560 03 3

Proof Editor: Andrew Clark

Acknowledgements

Sunderland Echo

Sunderland Central Library
(Local Studies)

Special Thanks

to

Pal Palmer

for the cartoons in this publication

Billy Bell
Archie Donaldson
Peter Gibson
Phil Hall
Judith Higgins
Joe Marsh
Stuart Miller
Monkwearmouth Local History Group
Newcastle Central Library
Jack Parkes
Arthur Ratcliffe, former Chief Operator, Roker Cinema
Martin Routledge
Sunderland Museum
Len H. Tindle, nephew of the late James H. Tindle Snr.
Margaret Tindle, widow of James H. Tindle Jnr.
University of Sunderland
Waples Collection
Kevin Wheelan
Joanne Wilson
John Yearnshire

Albert Anderson

Introduction

It is not within anyone's scope to tell the real story of Sunderland's cinemas. That lies in the personal memories of everyone of us whoever went to "The Pictures' when the town centre could boast a cinema on every corner and every suburb could boast its own local picture hall. Since 1896 Sunderland can claim to have had more than thirty cinemas and other moving picture halls - today we have three venues.

During my years of working in local cinemas as a projectionist I was fortunate enough to meet many people who had first hand experience of the transition from silence to sound and other technical advances. Through their stories and recollections I developed a valuable insight and undying interest in the cinema, and Sunderland's contribution to "The Greatest Entertainment The World Has Ever Seen".

The knowledge I gained inspired me to put this tribute together. All I can hope for is that my book and its unique photographs will answer many questions and give older readers many hours of pleasure while reminiscing about the town's picture halls. It will also give the younger cinemagoer of today an idea of what it was like before television and today's multi-screen complex.

Albert Anderson

Diary of Events

1859: DIORAMA shown at The Arcade Rooms in High Street.

1872: Opening of Victoria Hall

1882: Avenue Theatre and Star Music Hall open.

1883: Victoria Hall Disaster. Hamilton's Diorama exhibited at Royal Theatre.

1891: Livermore Bros. open Palace Theatre.

1896: Tussaud Exhibition presents Sunderland's first moving picture show.

1899: Olympia opens.

1901: Victoria Hall starts regular moving picture shows.

1904: Olympia presents moving pictures on the Olympiagraph. Villiers Street Institute presents moving pictures.

1906: Monkwearmouth Picture Hall opens. Royal Theatre shows moving pictures for first time.

1907: Pavilion opens. Empire Theatre opens. Wheat Sheaf Hall (Cora) becomes cinema.

1908: James H. Tindle exhibits moving pictures at the Avenue Theatre. Villette Hall (later Villette Cinema) presents regular picture shows.

1909: Hamilton's Flickerless Pictures at Palace.

1910: New Electric Theatre (Central) opens. Olympia closes down.

1911: Wheat Sheaf Hall becomes the Cora. Villette opens. Star cinema opens.

1912: Villiers Electric Theatre opens, along with the Theatre de Luxe, Savoy, Picture House and West End Kinema.

1913: Gem, Millfield, Gaiety, Queen's Hall Kinema, all open.

1914: Picture House presents *Morning Scenes on Roker Beach*.

1915: The Havelock and Roker cinemas open.

1916: Star cinema in Whitburn Street destroyed by Zeppelin raid. Monkwearmouth Picture Hall becomes Bridge Cinema.

1917: Central closes down, along with the Queen's Hall Kinema and Theatre de Luxe.

1919: Bridge Cinema becomes the Bromarsh.

1920: Victory opens.

1924: Gem closes down, along with the Pavilion.

1928: Villette and West End Kinema close down.

1929: Havelock presents *The Singing Fool* the town's first 'talkie'.

1931: *All Quiet on the Western Front* is given its North East premiere at the Empire.

1932: Regal opens and the Avenue closes down.

1935: Marina opens.

1936: Opening of the Plaza.

1937: Opening of the Ritz and Regent cinemas.

The Havelock illuminated with blue, green and red neon lights.

1940: Royal becomes a cinema.

1941: Victoria Hall destroyed by enemy landmine. Victory also destroyed in air raid.

1943: King's and Bromarsh destroyed by enemy bombing.

1947: Sunday opening approved after local referendum.

1956: Palace closes down.

1958: Gaiety and Villiers close.

1959: Cora, Savoy and Millfield close down.

1960: Empire becomes town's Civic Theatre.

1961: Roker and Regent close.

1963: Havelock and Marina close.

1966: Picture House closes.

1968: Plaza closes.

1969: Opening of Studios One & Two in High Street East.

1974: ABC (Ritz) closes temporarily for conversion to twin screens (now the Cannon).

1975: Odeon (Regal) closes for conversion to triple screen cinema (now Bingo).

1976: Roker building demolished.

1977: Fairworld takes over Studios One & Two.

1982: Odeon closes down.

1995: Screen on the River opens on St. Peter's Campus.

The Inventors

We know that Marconi developed the Wireless into practical use as long ago as 1895, that John Logie Baird transmitted the first ever Television pictures in 1926, although the images were crude and flickering, the principal of television had been proved and Baird believed that the invention could one day turn every home into a moving picture theatre. American multi-inventor Thomas Alva Edison gave us the phonograph in 1877, and in fact erected the first ever moving picture studio in the garden of his New Jersey home, where such famous celebrities as Buffalo Bill Cody and Annie Oakley were filmed. Many inventions over the years can be put down to many such individuals – not so cinema. For this – 'The greatest form of entertainment the world has ever seen' – came as a result of the discoveries and inventions of many men the world over.

In 1833 an English mathematician named W.G. Horner invented the ZOETROPE or Wheel of Life, which gave to pictures an appearance of movement. The apparatus took the form of a huge, hollow cylinder, which on the inside of the bottom section was arranged a series of painted images showing the successive stages in the movement of say a galloping horse, walking man, forms of transport and other moving objects.

Fifteen years later William Hamilton, eldest of four brothers of Scottish descent, founded the PANORAMA, known later as Hamilton's DIORAMA. Dioramas were in the form of giant vertical scrolls upon which were painted and illuminated scenes. These were slowly unwound to give beautiful panoramic views with musical accompaniment. The Hamilton's are credited with the founding of the travelling Diorama, which made their first appearance in the fairgrounds of England in 1848.

They toured the country's fairgrounds and theatres for more than half a century during which time the Hamilton's formed strong links with Sunderland. Their first visit to the town came in 1859 when they leased the old Arcade Rooms in High Street East for a short season. This was a huge success, and as a result Hamilton's Dioramas adopted Sunderland as the most popular venue on the circuit. On Friday 15th June 1883 the Diorama opened at the Royal Theatre in Bedford Street under the patronage of the Mayor, Alderman Wayman and leading civic figures. The hall on that opening night was packed to capacity, and the audience sat enthralled as the beauties of Venice, Rome, London and Paris unfolded before their eyes. Little did they know that the following day, in a hall not two hundred yards from where they were seated, a catastrophe of such magnitude that even today the results are difficult to accept as fact, would take place ... on a warm midsummer day in June, one hundred and eighty three of the town's children were to perish in the Victoria Hall Disaster.

It was the Victoria Hall in Toward Road, standing like a giant Mausoleum to the memory of the Disaster victims, that introduced the 'moving picture' show to the people of Sunderland, when on the 4th May 1896 the visiting Tussaud Exhibition gave local audiences their first glimpse of a new and sensational kind of entertainment ... living pictures.

The possibility that the mainly working class audience witnessed the first ever picture show to be seen in the provinces came to light in 1935 when Percival Craig, then living in retirement at Southend-on-Sea after working for many years in the theatres and cinemas of Sunderland, made the claim on the town's behalf. In a letter to the *Sunderland Echo* he challenged a claim made in the *Radio Times* on behalf of the Argyle Theatre in Birkenhead. The claim was that the Animated Photographs shown there in November 1896 were the first to be seen in the provinces. Rebuking the claim Mr. Craig said: "I believe Sunderland can claim that distinction, as I introduced them at Victoria Hall on 4th May 1896."

Following up that claim we turn to the *Sunderland Echo* of 5th May 1896, where we find a report of that historic occasion:

"All who watched the recent developments in photography, as well as those who would be entertained by the latest forms of amusements, will be interested to know that the ANIMATOGRAPH was shown yesterday at the Tussaud Exhibition in the Victoria Hall. Briefly described, the instrument projects a picture onto a screen, the figures of which are life size. These become animated in such a remarkable manner that it is easy to imagine that they are living people seen through a transparency. To describe one scene ... a burlesque on Trilby ... Svengali struts onto stage, followed by Trilby, who he proceeds to hypnotize. Other characters join in and execute a sort of dance in which finally the whole of the characters make their entrance every movement being exactly reproduced.

An advertisement from the *Weekly Echo & Times* for the first appearance of moving pictures in Sunderland.

Other scenes are: 'An Operation in a Dentist's chair', 'Blacksmiths at work in a Forge', 'Ejection of a disorderly person from a Public House', 'An American Lynching Scene', 'A Rescue from a Fire', and various interesting episodes. As Mr. Percival Craig who introduced the invention remarked: "The capabilities of the invention are limitless, there being nothing to prevent such events as say, a Royal Wedding, a Coronation, or even a battle being faithfully reproduced for the benefit of those who are not there to witness them. This latest addition to the programme, which also includes a Ladies Band, is likely to prove a very strong attraction."

Although forty years on from the birth of moving pictures, in 1935 little was known about the early development of the Kinematograph. With so many pioneers from different parts of the world working on its perfection and commercial possibilities, recording their progress was virtually impossible. Since then however a great deal of research has been carried out on the subject, and we are now able to trace with a great deal of certainty the important stages in its development.

Was Percival Craig right in his assertion that Sunderland was the first provincial venue for the moving picture show? The following synopsis of the earliest demonstrations in Kinematography answers our question.

Date	Inventor	Venue	
10th January 1888	Augustin Le Prince	Wood Lane, Leeds	Private Audience
22nd March 1895	Lumiere Bros.	Lyon, France	Private Audience
June 1895	J.R. Rudge	Bath, Y.M.C.A	Private Audience
July 1895	Birt Acres	Hedley Highstone	Private Audience
October 1895	Robert Paul	Hetton Gardens	Private Audience
23rd April 1896	Lumiere Bros.	London Polytechnic	Public Audience
23rd April 1896	Thomas Edison	Koster & Bials, New York U.S.A	Public Audience
28th April 1896	Tussaud Exhibition	Newcastle-upon-Tyne	Public Audience
4th May 1896	Tussaud Exhibition	Sunderland	Public Audience

From this list we can concede that the claim made on Sunderland's behalf, easy to believe at the time, has since been proved to be inaccurate.

Victoria Hall and in the foreground the monument to the 183 children who died during a matinee in 1883.

In November 1978 John George Stamp, once a well known figure in the Boldon, Seaburn and Southwick areas of Sunderland, recalled the day his mother took him to Victoria Hall to see that first picture show. This is the only first hand account one will find of the occasion, and is worth recording here.

He says, "I can well remember going with my mother to see the show. I was ten years old at the time, and we all thought how wonderful it was, even though the movements were very jerky. I am now ninety-two and you can be assured that I have followed the progress of the films and cinemas in Sunderland and district as the years have rolled by. I cannot recall seeing any more moving pictures in the years between 1896 and the Bromarsh opening about ten years later, after which they all opened."

Even though Mr. Stamp could not recall seeing any more pictures during that time, there were many to be seen.

The Livermore Brothers were the first to recognize the commercial possibilities of the 'moving picture' show in Sunderland. While the town's Avenue Theatre in Gillbridge Avenue, and the Royal in Bedford Street offered their patrons only snatches of the new medium, Livermore's Palace Theatre in High Street West offered audiences regular picture shows as part of their cine–variety policy, a system which was to become synonymous with local entertainment.

In July 1898 Edison's Royal Life Size Pictures (no connection with Thomas Alva Edison the American inventor) attracted large audiences to the Palace, with scenes from the Spanish-American War, and scenes of Gladstone's funeral.

Towards the end of 1896, most Music Halls and Theatres were equipped with projection machines, and although nothing concrete in the way of evidence is available it is possible that the Livermore Brothers exhibited moving pictures at the Palace at that time. Other theatres ran by them in the north, including the Bradford Palace often presented moving pictures in 1896. These films were of a short duration, known as 'chasers out', and other shorts usually of topical or local interest.

Today when the subject matter of films often causes some concern, it is worth noting that as far back as 1898 observers were warning of the threat to public morality the new entertainment posed. One such warning appeared in August 1898 in the pages of the *Sunderland Citizen*, and with it we got our first film critic!

"The Cinematograph. This is a most extraordinary invention, but I think the inventor (s) will be almost regretting that he ever produced it, since instead of being used for the improvement and advancement of mankind, it has hitherto been used for exhibitions of a most degrading nature. The prize-fight was bad enough, but 'The Bride's First Night' and such like exhibitions were outrageous. A friend of mine went to both. He went especially to see the effect upon the people. The effect was so vile that he assured me he doubted whether any decent working man would ever dare to admit to his children or women-folk that he had been there. Is there really no way to stop these things? We prohibit prize-fighting by law, we also prohibit public indecency. Have we not the power to prohibit exhibitions which are life size and amount to the same thing? Surely these are things for the Watch Committee to watch."

I wonder, was it really a 'friend' who shared 'The Bride's First Night'.

At the turn of the nineteenth century moving pictures were not seen as a threat to the legitimate theatre. They were regarded by most as a novelty, a seven day wonder. Even the legendary Richard Thornton, one of the true pioneers of the cinema in Sunderland refused to believe that this was where the future lay, till well after the turn of the century. However, he did present news items on the Bioscope at his theatres in Newcastle, Gateshead, South Shields, West Hartlepool, and of course Sunderland. In July 1899 scenes from that year's Cup Final between Derby County and Sheffield United were shown at Thornton's Avenue Theatre in Gillbridge Avenue and his Royal Theatre in Bedford Street. The People's Palace Theatre, where all the great Musical Hall artistes such as Charles Coburn ('The Man Who Broke The Bank at Monte Carlo'), Albert Chevalier, Charlie Chaplin, Dan Leno, and Vesta Tilley had appeared, also supplemented variety with moving pictures.

Victoria Hall

Ironically it was the Victoria Hall, scene of the disaster of 1883, and venue for the town's first picture show in 1896, which blazed the trail of the twentieth century cinema. For the first week of 1900 this hall with the 'evil reputation' presented what were proclaimed to be "The Most Beautiful Animated Pictures" ever seen in Sunderland, "A Triumph of Animated Photography, 10,000 pictures of the Boer War and our Navy".

The North American Animated Picture Company, under the guidance of Ralph Pringle made the first of many visits in 1906. On 24th April that year the NAAPC presented a French version of *The Life of Christ – From Birth to Resurrection*. With a running time of seventy five minutes, this was the longest film to be seen in Sunderland at that time. Directed by Alice Guy-Blanche for Lumiere this film saw Christ depicted on the screen for the very first time. Availability of films at times could not keep pace with demand and quite often there would be an acute shortage of American and home produced pictures. When this occurred, films would be imported from the continent, especially France, and an interpreter employed to read the foreign titles, and explain the plot. Back in those early years of the twentieth century, many of the audience perhaps were unable to read, and to others with poor eyesight, glasses would be a luxury that they could not afford. It was not unusual for someone who could not read to be accompanied by a person who could, and read the sub-titles out loud as they appeared on the screen.

One of the most popular of these 'lecturers' as they became known was Phil Roby, a slightly built man with a withered left arm who was in great demand, and an attraction in his own right.

Other visiting exhibitors included Sidney Carter and his New Century Pictures between 1907-1908, and local pioneers Holden & Midgeley, who in 1910 opened a new season "revealing the world in pictures" with special added varieties.

Towards the end of the February 1900 the Victoria Hall had been put up for sale on the open market. Anticipating the contribution such a building would make towards the public amenities of the town, the local corporation entered into negotiations for its purchase. These negotiations took over three years to complete, and finally in February 1903 the hall was bought for £8,000, considerably less than the reserved price.

It took another three years and an estimated cost of £30,000 to carry out modernization plans. These included the addition of two new halls where dinners and dances could be held with accommodation for one thousand people, and at the south end of the building would be a suite of luxury reception rooms for the more important functions. Electric lighting was installed throughout, and a giant organ built by local experts S.H. Vincent added to the newly decorated auditorium. The New Victoria Hall opened on 7th November 1906 with a

performance by the Sunderland Philharmonic Society, assisted by the world famous Halle Orchestra.

Under the guidance of the local authority a revitalized Victoria Hall continued for several years in its picture pioneering role, with only the very best in moving pictures being brought to the town. Many world famous celebrities appeared in person there, including Arthur Conan Doyle, Dame Clara Butte, and many more. The Victoria Hall was destroyed by an enemy landmine on the 15th April 1941.

The Victoria Hall lying in ruins after the air raid.

Olympia

By far the biggest local attraction between 1897-1907 was the Olympia Exhibition Hall in Borough Road, opened to mark the Jubilee of Queen Victoria, and situated on a site later occupied by the Regal Cinema and Rink Ballroom. The Richardson Brothers of Kelloe took over the lease at Olympia in 1899, turning it into a giant Pleasuredrome with roundabouts, gondolas and a free menagerie, and the best in Circus entertainment.

For the week commencing 25th September 1899 Olympia presented 'at enormous expense' leading circus performers Waller Sanger, Thomas Henry Culleen and Hugh Dempsey. Later that year the Fosset Family appeared. This legendary circus family included Thomas ... The Mad Poet, Emma ... England's greatest saddle rider, and Robert Fosset Jnr., billed as the country's premier jockey act. Tradition dies hard in the circus world, so today nearly one hundred years on Sir Robert Fosset's circus still makes regular visits to the town.

As an added attraction to the circus entertainment in December 1899, the Richardsons announced the special engagement of Edison George's Special War Pictures, described as "a most realistic and effective series of living photographs."

Commenting on the special performance given for the benefit of local reserve volunteers, under the patronage of the Mayor, Alderman Dix, the *Sunderland Echo* said:

"There was a large audience at Olympia last night, the attraction being Edison George's War Pictures and scenes in the Transvaal. While the pictures were being shown, the Olympian band played patriotic songs, with the audience joining in most heartily."

Prior to taking over Olympia the Richardson Brothers could boast little or no experience of the entertainment business. The eldest, Matt, left home at the age of sixteen to become a grocery assistant in Darlington. Within ten years he owned his own business which became a thriving concern. Gradually however he became more and more interested in fairground entertainment. In 1897 he was joined by his brother and together they concentrated their efforts in that direction.

Under their guidance Olympia became the most popular place of entertainment on Wearside. Open from 11 am to 11 pm daily, it offered a wide selection of amusements from roundabouts, switchbacks, and sideshows, there was also a twice nightly stage show featuring popular artistes of the day.

Olympia continued to enjoy enormous success and in 1906 it was announced that the building would be completely modernized. Proper flooring would be laid, bare walls were to be hidden by wainscotting, and other improvements would be made to make the building suitable for a wider range of entertainment. Attractive as

A large crowd gathers outside the Olympia at the turn of the century. In December 1899 the Olympia screened Edison George's Special War Pictures of the Boer War.

the plans were, the death knell for Olympia was already sounding. Business began to falter as a wider range of entertainments became available to the masses. A newly liberated community began flocking to the more luxurious setting of modern plush seated theatres which had sprung up in the town centre spearheaded by the King's in Crowtree Road (24th December 1906), the Empire (1st July 1907) and the long established Avenue in Gillbridge Avenue. Not only Olympia floundered, the Palace too suffered a decline in popularity. Time however would see the Palace survive the competition posed by the Empire, and go on to become one of the town's longest running cinemas.

Even the introduction of regular 'moving picture' shows on the Olympiagraph in 1904 failed to attract attendances large enough to guarantee its future as the opposition grew stronger. It held its own against the theatre, which for the best part of the Victorian age was a socially exclusive media, but the threshold of the twentieth century was the launching pad for an entertainment the like of which the world had never seen. The first decade of the century saw most theatres and music halls equipped with cinematograph machines of some description and the many short films produced since Lumiere's *Watering the Gardener* in 1896 were a popular added attraction. These films were known as 'chasers out' and had a basic formula. The policeman would chase the villain, while the dog chased the policeman, with more joining in the chase as the film progressed. The Olympia closed down in 1910, and twenty two years later Black's Regal – a byword in cinema luxury was built on the site.

Villiers Street Institute

(Not to be confused with the Villiers Theatre)

The year 1904 was a key one in the development of the cinema in Sunderland ... it was then that the first regular venue for the 'moving picture' show only was established. This was in the old Villiers Street Institute, the oldest existing building where such shows were held and where between 1904-1908 the Royal Canadian Animated Picture Company, assisted by the East End Prize Band played to packed houses nightly. Most of the films shown would have a running time of about ten or fifteen minutes, and were mainly documentaries of local and topical interest. Most popular of the 1906 programme were 'The Launching of the Dreadnought' by H.M. The King, the Sunderland v Aston Villa and Everton v Newcastle United football matches, and 'The Arrival of Japanese Sailors on the Tyne'. In 1905 the Institute advertised "10,000 Animated Pictures which can only be seen at the Institute."

Other venues for the occasional picture shows were the Villette Hall (later the Villette Cinema) where the Chicago Animated Company were regular visitors, and the Sans Street Mission at the bottom of High Street East. Sixty years later the Mission showed films under its modern name of Studios One & Two. Only part of the Villiers Street Institute building is still standing.

Sunderland had a variety of entertainments prior to the First World War, including Thiel's Arcadia under the Holey Rock which featured the Roker Pierrots, the Cosy Gardens at Seaside Lane Terminus, Jumbles Pavilion also under the Holey Rock, and the Egyptian Hall of Mysteries and Penny Gaff in High Street.

Bromarsh

(Monkwearmouth Picture Hall, Bridge Cinema, Black's Picture Palace)

Sunderland got its first permanent cinema on 14th May 1906 when George Black senior, head of a family which for many years ahead was to have a dominating influence on local and national entertainment, converted the former St. Stephen's Chapel in Bonnersfield into the Monkwearmouth Picture Hall. Prior to this the disused place of worship had been the home of a Waxworks Exhibition, attracting large numbers of visitors to the Mysteries of the East.

George Black and his three sons, George, Alfred, and Edward ran the Monkwearmouth Picture Hall under the name of the British Animated Picture Company. Firmly established as opening in May 1906, and claimed by the Blacks as being the first permanent cinema north of Birmingham, there is evidence to suggest that moving pictures were put on as early as 1904 as an added attraction to the Waxworks.

Old George died in 1911, and George Jnr., Alfred and Edward took over the reins of the cinema.

The opening programme at the Monkwearmouth Picture Hall included one showing the launching of the *Mauretania*, a great attraction for a shipbuilding town like Sunderland. Even though real live launches were a common sight on the busy River Wear, great crowds made their way to the new cinema at the north end of the bridge, and the former chapel which had accommodated much smaller congregations in worship was filled to capacity nightly with the first generation of cinemagoers.

When George Black opened the Monkwearmouth

The building plan of Monkwearmouth Picture Hall.

Picture Hall it really was a family run cinema. George, the eldest of his three sons operated the hand cranked kinematograph, Alfred took the money at they pay-box from patrons who had to sit on hard wooden seating in old chapel pews, and Edward the youngest of the brothers who were all at the time teenagers, wrote out all the

Despite the advertising material adorning the facade, evidence of Black's Picture Palace's religious origins can still be detected.

prologues for the silent films which were projected on to a large white sheet hanging at the front of the hall.

The second week's programme featured the thriller *The Attack On The Agent* supported by several shorts. On 22nd May 1906 the *Sunderland Echo* observed: "The Black's Animated Picture Company are making an impression with the entertainment they are providing at the Picture Hall, formerly St. Stephen's Chapel in Bonnersfield. Performances are given nightly, and last night the programme was entertaining and pleasing. One picture, *An Irish Eviction* is particularly fine, *An Opium Eater's Dream* and *A Moonlight Dream* are attractive pictures, and a *British Cruiser in a Storm* is another interesting subject. There are also numerous comic pictures."

Other pictures which attracted large audiences during the early weeks after opening were *Oliver Twist*, *The Child Stealers*, *The New Woman* and *The Games At Athens*. Even in those early pioneering days of the cinema the Black Brothers showed exceptional foresight at the Monkwearmouth Picture Hall. As early as 1907 they anticipated the Cinematograph Act of 1910 by isolating the projection equipment from the audience, and originating the 'twice nightly' shows.

The enormous success of the Monkwearmouth Picture Hall enabled the Black Brothers to expand, in 1909 they built the Gateshead Palace, and took over the Palace in Hartlepool. The following year The Royal Blyth and the Boro at North Shields came under their control. By 1912 the brothers controlled a chain of twelve cinemas in the area.

Early in 1918 they took over the King's in Crowtree Road, and the following year George negotiated the sale of shares in several of their cinemas. Including, the Boro at Wallsend, Palace at Gateshead, Grand at Byker, Boro at North Shields, Palace at Hartlepool, and the King's in Crowtree Road, at an estimated price of £250,000.

The opening of the Monkwearmouth Picture Hall and its immediate success could not have come at a worse time for local theatrical interests, for at the time no-one visualised the rapid rise in popularity of moving pictures, which in Sunderland alone would see the opening of eighteen picture halls in the space of ten years.

In 1916 the Monkwearmouth Picture Hall became known as the Bridge Cinema, the name it retained till 1919 when it was re-named the Bromarsh after being taken over by the Marshall Brothers, hence its name, Bromarsh being an anagram in part of MARSHall BROthers.

George Black broke his ties with the family interest in local entertainment in 1928 and moved to London as Director of the General Theatre Corporation, and in 1933 took over Moss Empires as joint managing director. Between the wars he was widely recognized as the most outstanding figure in Music Hall, with his Crazy Gang shows at the London Palladium bringing back all the

A view of Black's Picture Palace across Wearmouth Bridge before the First World War.

BLACK'S

Picture Palace,

MONKWEARMOUTH.

Proprietors - - - - - Brothers BLACK.

The most Up-to-date Picture and Variety Hall in Sunderland.

TWICE NIGHTLY, 7 AND 9.

Matinee on Saturday at 3.

FRONT CIRCLE, 6d. ; BACK CIRCLE, 4d.
Do. PIT, 2d. ; Do. PIT 3d.

This is the Premier Picture Hall in the North of England, and was established in 1904 by the late Mr. George Black. Run in conjunction with the Borough Theatre, North Shields ; Palace Theatre, West Hartlepool ; Picture Palace, Gateshead ; and the Tivoli, South Shields.

atmosphere of the old music hall days.

Alfred and Edward opened the Regal in 1932, the most luxurious of all their cinemas. Four years later in 1936 Edward gave up his interest in the cinema chain and moved into cinema production with Max Ostrer at Gainsborough Studios, where he produced many successful films for that company, Gaumont British, London Films, Twentieth Century Fox and Rank.

The Bromarsh was destroyed by enemy bombing on 24th May 1943. The last film shown was *49th Parallel* starring Leslie Howard.

Royal Theatre

The Royal Theatre in Bedford Street was opened by Roxby & Beverley in December 1855, and proprietors in later years included Stuart Henry Bell (1872), G. Goddart Wyatt, C. Hall & E.D. Davis (1876), and Edward Moss, founder of the Moss Empire in 1833.

Hamilton's Diorama was first seen at the Royal on 15th June 1883, the eve of the Victoria Hall Disaster.

In 1889 Richard Thornton took over as director of Sunderland Theatres Ltd., and in 1906 the Royal put on animated pictures for the first time. The programme included a film of the Britt v Nelson World Championship fight ... the first recorded boxing film to be seen in Sunderland. At this time Thornton also ran the Avenue Theatre in Gillbridge Avenue, and in September 1906 he stood alongside that legendary music hall artiste Vesta Tilley as she laid the foundation stone of the Empire Theatre, the 'jewel in the crown' of his vast theatre chain.

Because of the recession the Royal closed down in 1933, becoming a boxing stadium shortly after. It re-opened as a cinema in November 1940 with Charles Laughton in *Ruggles of Red Gap* and *Bluebeard's Eighth Wife* starring Cary Grant. During World War Two it put on Sunday evening concerts which were very popular with local audiences.

Right: A rainy day in Bedford Street, while the audience inside the Royal were enjoying *South Pacific.*

Above: The Royal Theatre today. A recent fire has left the building without a roof and with an uncertain future.

Left: The Roast Potato Man who sold his wares outside the Royal.

Scala
(Pavilion, Star Music Hall)

In 1857 the Assembly Rooms in Upper Sans Street (near Coronation Street) were opened and twenty years later the Italian style building became the Star Music Hall, with a Signor Durland as proprietor.

'Signor Durland' hid the identity of George Thomas Rudland who was born in 1834, place not known. As a youth he became a scene painter for circuses and travelled the continent of Europe studying art, in particularly France and Italy. He was attracted to the Italian style of painting and consequently was addressed as Signor Rudland. In 1882 he arrived in Sunderland from Birmingham where he is reported to have been connected with the Alhambra Circus. His brother Henry was a builder in Sunderland, and when George intimated that he was about to try his luck in the town as a Music Hall proprietor, his brother did not wish to be identified with the project and insisted he change his name to 'Signor Durland', an anagram of Rudland.

Signor Durland took over the Assembly Rooms and opened up as the Star Music Hall on 26th December 1882, with Mr. J. Fairly the 'Lion Comique' topping the bill of music hall artistes. The auditorium could accommodate 1000 people, 500 in the pit and pit stalls, 400 in the gallery, and about 100 in the boxes. There were two main entrances from Sans Street, and a Gallery door.

Only one year after opening the Star was badly damaged by fire during the performance on Saturday 16th August 1883. A huge gasoline (or sunlight burner) which hung from the roof was being turned up during the interval when a surge of gas flame ignited from the

Star Music Hall

roof timbers and in a very short time the roof was ablaze from end to end. The Signor announced from the stage that "something had gone wrong" and asked the audience to leave at once in an orderly manner, assuring them that everything was under control. The audience rose en masse and left without any sign of panic.

With the opening of the doors however the inrush of air fanned the flames into a blazing inferno. One hour after the outbreak, the roof collapsed, all the decorative fittings were destroyed including the open boxes and their handsome mirrors. Only the gallery was saved from total destruction. The artistes who had to evacuate their dressing rooms still dressed in sock and buckskin, mingled with the crowds which packed the surrounding streets. By the time the fire was extinguished at 10 pm, only the rear and side walls along with the gallery seating remained. While the Signor was insured against damage, the properties were not included, and he never fully recovered financially from having to make good the loss. His brother George would not assist him, and although the Star Music Hall was restored and made functional, financial embarrassment forced the Signor to vacate the premises in 1882. It was then put to use as a Salvation Army Barracks until 1906.

When the Salvation Army moved to their new barracks in 1906, the building was taken over by Lough & Richardson, who re-opened it as the Pavilion Cinema on

Signor Durland

Above: An advert for a picture show at the Pavilion in 1907.

11th February 1907, under the patronage of Colonel Vaux. The new cinema could seat 500 patrons, and the first films shown were *Uncle Tom's Cabin*, *The Village Fire Brigade* and *Dead Men Tell No Tales*. It was later re-named the Scala, the name it was known by till it closed in 1924, it then lay empty till 1930 when it was purchased by Charles Jolly for his motor garage. When Jolly took

possession the wooden figures which had occupied the exterior alcoves were discovered in the building, but in poor condition. They were given to someone to restore and the opinion was expressed that they had originally been wooden figureheads from sailing ships of the Wear.

Above: The building shortly before its demolition to make way for a new road.

Gibb McLaughlin

Gibb McLaughlin was born in Sunderland and became a stage monologuist before entering films. He was a master of disguise as well as a fine character actor. Some of his best known films were: *Carnival* (1921), *Nell Gwynn* (1924), *Farmer's Wife* (1927), *The Temperance Fete* (1929), *Sally in Our Alley* (1931), *Private Life of Henry VIII* (1932), *The Thirteenth Candle* (1933), *No Funny Business* (1933), *The Scarlet Pimpernel* (1934), *Where There's A Will* (1936) *Mr. Reeder in Room 13* (1940), *My Learned Friend* (1943), *Caesar and Cleopatra* (1945), *Oliver Twist* (1948), *The Card* (1952), *Hobson's Choice* (1954), *Sea Wife* (1957) and many more.

The *Sunderland Echo* of 10th July 1961 reported:

Death Of Wearside Actor

A man who brought pleasure to millions of people over a period of 60 years, the Sunderland-born character actor Gibb McLaughlin, has died in a London hospital. Mr McLaughlin would have been 82 on Wednesday of next week.

Mr McLaughlin, whose most recent television appearances were in the Charlie Drake and "Dixon of Dock Green" series, leaves no family but he has a niece, Mrs W. Baister, at present living at Cleadon. He was twice married.

He was born in the Deptford Road premises of Hartley's Glass Works, of which his father was manager, and was a member of All Saints' Church, Monkwearmouth, before he left Wearside to seek a career on the stage.

Gibb McLaughlin (seated) in a scene from *Hobson's Choice.*

Cora
(Coronation Picture Palace, Wheat Sheaf Hall)

The Wheat Sheaf Hall at the bottom of Southwick Road was taken over by Lough & Richardson on 1907 for the presentation of moving pictures. Their tenancy lasted only a year, then it came under the control of James H. Tindle who gave it the more explanatory title of Wheat Sheaf Picture Hall, in 1911 it became the Coronation Picture Palace (marking the Coronation of George V), and after 1913 it was simply known as the Cora.

Between 1908 - 1920 James H. Tindle also controlled the Empress at Horden, the Kino, Jarrow, and the Albert Hall, Edinburgh. After his death the running of the circuit was taken over by his eldest son, also named James. The Cora was Sunderland's second smallest cinema (the Gem in Clockwell Street, Southwick was the smallest). It was always described, perhaps unfairly as a 'flea pit', a reputation which it inherited after it was closed temporarily in 1930 by the local health authority. It re-opened shortly after with talking pictures, unlike many other small halls which closed with the coming of sound.

James Tindle Jnr. died in 1948 with only the Cora remaining of the small circuit, and this came under control of his widow Margaret until closure in 1959. Mrs.

Tindle was a popular and highly respected figure to the Cora's regulars, and the last of the independent cinema owners. She died in 1993 when in her late nineties.

The late Len H. Tindle, nephew of James Tindle Snr., then living in New South Wales told me about his uncle. "I worked with my uncle for a number of years at the old Avenue Theatre and the Cora. He was a fair and just man, very interested in all aspects of photography. When flickering appeared in films it was most annoying and difficult to concentrate on the story. My uncle vowed he would rectify the fault, and in time did make an improvement on the flickering wheel of the projector.

"The projector was hand cranked in those days and I recall them well ... collar and tie off, shirt sleeves rolled up in a box 6' x 6' x 8' high all encased in sheet metal. The heat from the arc lamps was intense created by the burning positive and negative carbons. No electric fans those days. I remember some of the forerunners of the sound-track talkies at the Cora, silent films with synchronized sound on disc. To give the audience some idea of the coming sound films we would play a Phonograph, and the song was:

The Cora Picture Palace during the 1930s.

Above: The staff and management of the Cora on their annual outing in the 1920s. Christine Norden's father was a bus driver and at one time drove the Cinema Star, one of Harry Tindle's buses.

James H. Tindle Snr.

When the fields are white with daisies, and roses bloom again
    Let the love flame in your heart more brightly burn
For I love you sweetheart only, so remember when you are lonely
    When the fields are white with daisies I'll return.

"A slide was put on the showing a young lady all in white in a field of daisies and a sailor pictured singing the song. Different slides were put on according to the words of the song, and we had to keep an ear to the music in order to change the slides.

"Uncle Jim had been a stage mimic, and he was very good, I heard him a few times when he visited our home. He was also for a time Sir Harry Lauder's touring manager, then he became a partner of Richard Thornton. He also ran a fleet of charabancs which were called Cinema Queen, Cinema Princess, and the Cinema Star. I recall them well. On a match day cousin Harry Tindle would take a charabanc up to Grangetown, I would be with him and we used to shout "This way to Roker Park, only 6d a trip." When we had a full load I would hang on the side and collect the fares. The charabancs were kept in a garage opposite the Miners Hall in Roker Avenue, just below the Roker cinema."

The Cora building stood for nearly twenty five years after closure before being demolished in September 1982.

Queuing up for the Cora under the watchful eye of 'Jimmy' Tindle.

Avenue Theatre & Opera House

Situated in Gillbridge Avenue the 1500 seated Avenue was opened by Richard Thornton on 30th October 1882 with a play called *The Guv'nor*. It occupied the site formerly occupied by Milburn's Varieties.

The farewell appearance of Sir Henry Irving, who made his professional stage debut at the Lyceum in Lambton Street in 1859, was given at the Avenue on 28th October 1904, and during 1907 - 1908 James H. Tindle exhibited the theatre's first moving pictures.

Although history pays tribute to the part played by the Blacks in the pioneering days of local cinema, it tends to ignore the part played by Tindle, a contemporary of the Blacks and no less a pioneer. While the Black family may have given us our first permanent cinema, it was Jimmy Tindle who gave us the Cora ... and who amongst us that ever saw a show in the Wheat Sheaf Hall will ever forget the experience!

It was Tindle's brother-in-law Richard Thornton who introduced him to the magic of moving pictures. At the turn of the century he engaged him to operate the Bioscopes that had been introduced in his vast chain of Empire theatres throughout England.

As a result of that experience Tindle became a fine technician, and was always recognized as such. Thornton opened the Empire Theatre in 1907 and as a result the Avenue suffered and although given a new lease of life through a cine-variety policy, drifted into a period of recession and eventually closed in 1932.

Opposition from the Empire gave Tindle the perfect opportunity to make full use of the knowledge he had gained at the handle of the Bioscope, and give credibility to an entertainment which he had great faith in ... but regarded by many as a mere novelty that would pass over, never offering a real challenge to the legitimate theatre.

The Avenue during its final week in 1932.

Richard Thornton

He obtained a lease on the Avenue in the summer of 1908 and re-opened it as a picture hall, where Tindle's pictures became a must on the itinerary of the first generation of Sunderland cinemagoers. The success of the Avenue enabled him to expand his cinema interests which began with the opening of the Wheat Sheaf Hall in 1908. In 1916 the famous serial *The Perils of Pauline* was shown. Unfortunately this popular theatre only lasted a few years after the introduction of talkies and closed down with a second rate review *Sunshine Sally* on 27th February 1932.

The building is now occupied in part by Vaux brewery.

Although now part of Vaux Brewery, the outline of the old Avenue Theatre can still be recognised.

Villette

The Villette Hall was used for moving picture shows in 1908 by the Chicago Animated Picture Company, and in 1911 it became the Villette Cinema, operated by the Villette Picture Company, with Dixon Scott as manager. The Villette closed down when talkies came in 1929, and the last film shown was *The Big Parade* starring Renee Adoree.

Right: An advert from the 1911 *Sunderland Year Book.*

Silents Only

The Villette was one of eight Sunderland cinemas that never made the transition to sound. The others being: Central, Gem, Scala, Queen's Hall Kinema, Star, Theatre de Luxe and West End Kinema.

THE NEW PICTURE HALL!

THE

"VILLETTE"

Villette Road, Hendon.

This Hall is now the Daintiest and Most Comfortable in the District and the Programmes shewn are only of the VERY BEST.

THE "VILLETTE" CATERS FOR EVERYONE

WHO WANTS A GOOD ENTERTAINMENT AT A LOW PRICE

BRING THE FAMILY!

Palace Theatre

The Palace Theatre was designed by Thomas Angelo Moore and opened by the Livermore Brothers in 1891. During 1906 the Palace was taken over by Rosen & Bliss, and in the same year a young Charlie Chaplin made an appearance in the *Mumming Birds*. It closed down due to strong competition from the newly built Empire in 1908 - 1909. Its saviours came in 1909 with the presentation of Hamilton's Flickerless Pictures.

From 1918 to 1948 the position of manager was held by Mrs. Gray, the only woman to hold such a position in those days. The success of the talkies saw the Palace close for two weeks in July 1930 for conversion to sound, and re-open with *Their Own Desire* starring Norma Shearer and *Navy Blues* with William Haynes in the starring role.

The Palace went the way of so many cinemas during the massive decline of the 1950s closing down on 1st December 1956 with *The Eddy Duchin Story* starring Tyrone Power.

Sunderland Leisure Centre now occupies the site.

A Gamp
for the Ladies

When people queued in the rain the management of the Palace (and also the King's) would send out umbrellas for the ladies.

The Palace Theatre circ. 1950.

The Palace interior.

New Electric Theatre
(Central ... 'Pop In')

Lough & Richardson who also ran the Star in Calvert Street and the Pavilion, opened the New Electric Theatre on 5th November 1910 and the first film shown was the comedy *Percy the Cowboy* supported by Pathe's Animated Gazette. Situated in Green Street on a site presently occupied by Marks & Spencer, it could seat approximately 250 patrons.

Like all other cinemas during the silent era the action on the screen was usually followed by descriptive musical

Above: The Marks & Spencer store now occupies the site on which the 'Pop In' once stood.

Left: A ticket from the Central.

Bring a PENNY and This Ticket
TO THE
CENTRAL PICTURE HALL
GREEN STREET (opposite Station)
On SATURDAY AFTERNOON,
at 2-30.   Doors open at 2 o'clock.

Grand Children's Performance.
Full Programme of the
World's Best Animated Pictures.

accompaniment and pretty basic sound effects. In the New Electric's case the films were accompanied by Cissy Bold on the piano, with sound effects for example like the rattling of half cocoanut shells for the sound of a galloping horse.

In 1912 the New Electric Theatre was re-named the Central, but from 1915 it was known simply as the 'Pop In' till its closure in 1919 when it became a billiard hall.

Empire Theatre

The Empire Theatre ... Thornton's 'jewel in the crown' ... was opened by the town's greatest impresario on 1st July 1907, only ten months after music hall legend Vesta Tilley had laid the foundation stone on 29th June 1906. Always regarded as a premier home of variety this most beautiful of theatres has not only during its ninety years history brought the best in live entertainment to the town, it also occupies a special place in the town's cinema history.

For several years after opening the Empire included Bioscope moving pictures as an extra to the music hall entertainment, these were a great and popular added attraction. In 1909 it screened that year's Grand National, the Sunderland v Sheffield United, and Sunderland v Preston North End Cup ties. The Coronation of King George V and Queen Mary was shown in June 1911, and in the July it advertised: 'The Only Stereoscopic Life Motion Pictures in their actual colours of nature. The Greatest wonder of the age can only be seen at the Empire. See 'London before the Coronation', London Illuminated', 'Coronation Procession at the Mall', and 'Peers going to the Abbey by Steamer'.

Other items of interest shown between 1911 - 1913 included the Investiture of the Prince of Wales at Caernarvon, the Sunderland v Aston Villa Cup Final at Crystal Palace, the Johnson v Jeffries fight, and the funeral of Buffalo Bill Cody.

The Empire Theatre's opening night bill on 1st July 1907. Moving pictures on the Bioscope are advertised as part of the entertainment. Vesta Tilley who laid the Empire's foundation stone topped the bill.

The imposing corner entrance of the Empire Theatre.

In the immediate post World War One years the Empire screened Charlie Chaplin's Keystone comedies, The Jack Johnson v Jess Willard Heavyweight title fight, and the D.W. Griffith classic *Birth of a Nation* which at three hours long was the longest picture yet seen in the town.

With the coming of sound in 1929 and the public's clamour for 'talking pictures', nothing but the best in the new medium was brought to the theatre, which set out on a long period of matinee performances, with live variety on the evenings. Among the best of their early talkies were *The Four Feathers* (1930), starring Fay Wray, Noah Beery, and Clive Brook, the North East premiere of the anti-war classic *All Quiet on the Western Front* (1931), *King of Jazz* with John Boles and the Paul Whiteman Orchestra, *Sky Devils* starring Spencer Tracy, and the Oscar-winning *Grand Hotel* featuring Greta Garbo, Joan Crawford and Wallace Beery.

Many of the performers who appeared on the Empire during its music hall/variety/revue years went on to become stars of the cinema screen and international celebrities. Charlie Chaplin and Stan Laurel in *Mumming*

Birds (1908), W.C. Fields made two appearances on the stage in 1908 and 1913, Elizabeth Risdon, a Hollywood co-star who appeared in many films including the romantic *Random Harvest* (1915), Jack Buchanan (1916), Will Fyffe (1918), Will Hay (1920), Eddie Polo, billed as 'The Famous American Cowboy Star' (1925).

Perhaps the smartest way of cashing in on the moving picture craze was put on at the Empire in February 1920, when Harry Burns presented the stage show *Making Movies*. This set out to show the public the actual taking and making of a film, in a real motion picture studio on the stage. Patrons were asked to come and see the complete studio, Movie Director, Camera Man, Handsome Juvenile, Vampire, and Angry Mob. Does Sunderland have a Charlie Chaplin, Mary Pickford, or Douglas Fairbanks? It may be you, here's your chance to become a picture star! See yourself on the screen they were told, Tears, Laughs, Screams, Howls, and Yells.

Above: George Formby ... number one at the box-office in the Second World War ... paid his first visit to the Empire in 1929, following in his father's footsteps who appeared there on many occasions. Also that year, Gracie Fields, arguably the greatest of our musical comedy stars, delighted local audiences with her appearance in Archie Pitt's *The Show's The Thing*. While in Sunderland 'Our Gracie' stopped the traffic in Fawcett Street when she visited Binns store to autograph copies of her latest record. That lovable duo Flanagan and Allen took second place to Florrie Forde's top billing in 1932, and the most famous cowboy of the silver screen Tom Mix, and his horse Tony, took the town by storm when they played the Empire.

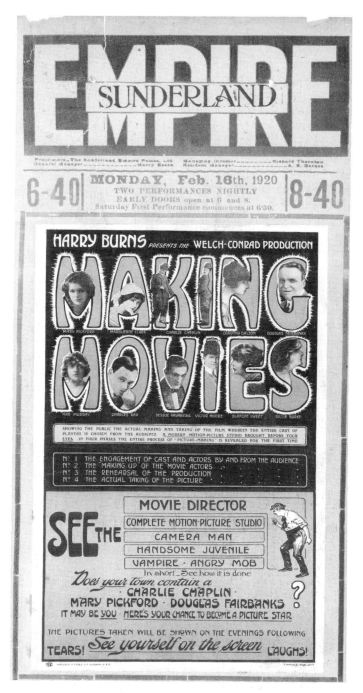

An Empire *Making Movies* bill from 1920.

After the Second World War several American film stars, who in all honesty had passed their 'sell by date', included the Empire on their British tour of the provinces. Among the most notable of these were Laurel & Hardy, John Boles (who had been the star of the film *King of Jazz*, shown at the theatre in 1931), singing boy star Bobby Breen, and the Nicholas Brothers, tap dancing stars of many Hollywood musicals.

The fifties and sixties saw the emergence of the pop star ... Frankie Vaughan, David Whitfield, Tommy Steele (who made his stage debut at the Empire in 1956), Cliff Richard and the Shadows, Helen Shapiro, and of course the Beatles come readily to mind. The most successful of these Frankie Vaughan, Tommy Steele, Cliff Richard, and the Beatles, went on to star in several films although not 'film stars' in the recognized way.

The Empire was taken over in 1960 by the local authority and re-named the Civic Theatre a name it retained for some time before once again becoming the Empire. Today it has its own Studio Cinema, which offers only the very best in big screen entertainment.

We cannot leave the Empire without paying tribute to Richard Thornton (1839-1922) described in 1909 as 'the most successful provider of public entertainment the North East of England has ever produced', a description that would be matched by George Black in later years.

A native of South Shields, he had very little education and went to work at an early age as a pit lad at St. Hilda's Colliery. At the age of thirty he played first violin at Marsden Grotto, and five years later was resident conductor of the Theatre Royal Orchestra at South Shields. He acquired property in Union Alley, North Shields, turning it into a first class music hall. The popularity of which enabled him to lease The Royal Theatre in Bedford Street, also to be run as a music hall. In partnership with Sir Edward Moss, founder of the Moss Empires, he bought the Royal Scotch Arms Hotel, Newcastle, and built the city's Empire Theatre. They were joined in partnership by Oswald Stoll, the combination being known in 1909 as the Moss, Stoll, Thornton and Allen Theatres controlling thirty six theatres nationwide. They controlled the Empire till 1933, when it came under Moss Empires with Sunderland's George Black as Managing Director.

The Empire Studio.

Above: George Black, Sunderland's greatest purveyor of entertainment, eldest brother of Alfred and Edward. George went to London in 1928 as Director of General Theatre Corporation. In 1933 he joined Moss Empires as joint managing director. Next to C.B. Cochrane he was the most outstanding figure in music hall between the wars.

The Films of Edward Black

Six years after opening the Regal with his brother Alfred, Edward Black, the youngest of the brothers, who once wrote out the prologues at the Monkwearmouth Picture Hall decided to go into production. Between 1938 and 1944 he produced a great number of popular films, featuring many of the great film stars of the day. Following is a list of his best known productions.

1937: *Young and Innocent* starring Nova Pilbeam
Oh Mr. Porter starring Will Hay
1938: *The Lady Vanishes* starring Margaret Lockwood
Convict 99 starring Will Hay
Bank Holiday starring Margaret Lockwood
Alf's Button Afloat starring Flanagan & Allen
Ask A Policeman starring Will Hay
1939: *Where's That Fire* starring Will Hay
The Frozen Limits starring Crazy Gang
A Girl Must Live starring Margaret Lockwood
Band Wagon starring Arthur Askey
1940: *Charley's Big Hearted Aunt* starring Arthur Askey
The Girl in The News starring Margaret Lockwood
Gas Bags starring Crazy Gang
1941: *Hi Gang* starring Bebe Daniels and Ben Lyon
The Ghost Train starring Arthur Askey
Cottage To Let starring John Mills
1942: *It's That Man Again* starring Tommy Handley
The Young Mr. Pitt starring Robert Donat
Uncensored starring Eric Portman
1943: *Bonnie Prince Charlie* starring Jack Hawkins
Dear Octopus starring Margaret Lockwood
We Dive At Dawn starring John Mills
Millions Like Us starring Patricia Roc
1944: *Waterloo Road* starring John Mills and Stewart Grainger
Fanny By Gaslight starring James Mason
2000 Women starring Patricia Roc and Flora Robson

Star

Not to be confused with the Star Music Hall, the Star Cinema was situated in Whitburn Street, Monkwearmouth, and was run by Lough & Richardson who also controlled the Central, and Pavilion. It was one of the smallest halls, with seating for about 300 patrons. They operated a 'penny and pass' system which meant retaining your ticket for your next visit, when you would present it at the pay-box and get in for a penny.

Its lease of life was very short, being destroyed during a Zeppelin raid on the town on the first of April 1916. That same night the transport offices at the Wheat Sheaf were also hit.

Right: An advert from *Sunderland Year Book* of 1912 for three of Lough & Richardson's local picture halls.

THE STAR AND CENTRAL
PICTURE   HALLS
AT THE STAR–"DEMONYTE," Two-Part Drama and others. DOT DRISCOLL, Child Vocalist.
CHRISTMAS DAY–TWO PERFORMANCES at 6.30 and 8.30.
AT THE CENTRAL–Last Part of "WHAT HAPPENED TO MARY," "The Burden Bearer," Drama, CHRISTMAS DAY AT THE CENTRAL–Special Programme at 6.30 and 8.30. Holiday Matinee on Boxing Day at 2.30. Entirely New Programme.
Usual Prices.

Above: The Christmas programme for The Star and Central in 1913.

When you are out on Pleasure Bent, and looking for **Good Pictures**
—— VISIT ——
The Star Picture Hall, Whitburn Street.
The Central Picture Hall, Green Street.
Also the PAVILION (Pictures & Varieties) SANS ST., SUNDERLAND

MR. E. R. LOUGH.

MR. J. E. RICHARDSON.

Lessees - Messrs. LOUCH and RICHARDSON.
Who show the World's Best Pictures all the year round.

Twice Nightly, 7 and 9.
And Grand Matinees for Children every Saturday Afternoon.

Entire change of Programme
TWICE WEEKLY.

Only the Best Pictures shown in First-class Style.

GO-AS-YOU-PLEASE COMPETITIONS every Friday night at the Pavilion, also at the Star every Saturday night.   Money Prizes.
POPULAR PRICES 2d, 3d, 4d, and 6d.

Above: Poster hoardings were one means by which local cinemas advertised forthcoming films. These particular ones were situated in Roker Avenue. The exact date can be traced by the films advertised. *Palais de Danse* played at the Roker Variety Theatre and the Picture House screened *Scaramouche* between 8th and 10th July 1929.

Villiers Electric Theatre

The Villiers holds the rare distinction of being the first purpose-built cinema in the town, as opposed to others we talked about previously which were converted from other buildings. A large cinema for its time, it was advertised as holding 1,000 patrons, and costing £4,000 to build. It was opened on 22nd January 1912 by Sunderland Amusements, and the first film shown was *The Great Mine Disaster*. Later on it was to be run in conjunction with the Roker in Roker Avenue, showing the same programme on the same night. It was a common sight in those days to see boys on cycles riding back and forth over Wearmouth bridge with reels of film for the twin cinemas.

Bob Spurs started at the Villiers as a sixteen year old and remained in the cinema business for forty five years, till retiring in 1976. In the heyday of the picture halls he managed all over the North East before joining the army where he saw service with the Cinematograph Corps, showing films to servicemen. In 1950 he joined Black's cinema chain and after a spell as relief manager, became manager of the Regal, Byker where he stayed for twenty two years. His only regret about the business was that the

The Villiers Electric Theatre
Villiers Street South.

The Latest and Best Equipped HALL in the District.

Tip-up Seats Throughout.

Accommodation for over **1,000** Persons.

TWICE NIGHTLY,
6·50 and 9.
MATINEE SATURDAYS
2·30.

No trouble or expense spared by the Directors to provide a High-class Entertainment

Prices—**6d., 4d., 2d.**

Box Office open 11 to 1 daily. Tel. 1504.

CHANGE OF PROGRAMME TWICE WEEKLY.

old days of cine-variety was over. He spoke for many members of the industry when he said on retiring, "Its the best business in the world ... I just wish I could be part of it again."

The Villiers closed down on 16th March 1958 with the Disney film *Rob Roy*.

Villiers Electric Theatre, the Bede Paint Works stood next door and Hudson Road School opposite.

Theatre De Luxe

The Theatre de Luxe stood opposite the old Town Hall in Fawcett Street, and was owned by A.G. Hamilton who also ran the Flickerless Pictures at the Palace. It opened on 29th April 1912 with the silent epic *Titanic*. Tea was served at afternoon matinees and patrons were entertained between films by the Bijou Orchestra. Opposition from the newly opened Havelock forced its closure in 1917.

Situated across the road to the Town Hall, the Theatre de Luxe remained open only five years

While the Town Hall has long gone the building that housed the Theatre de Luxe is still going strong.

The ten most popular film stars, male and female, according to the findings of the Bernstein questionnaire to British filmgoers in 1937 were:

Gary Cooper	Norma Shearer
Clark Gable	Mryna Loy
Charles Laughton	Greta Garbo
Robert Taylor	Ginger Rogers
Ronald Colman	Claudette Colbert
William Powell	Shirley Temple
Franchot Tone	Jessie Matthews
George Arliss	Kay Francis
Fredric March	Merle Oberon
Robert Donat	Loretta Young

Comparisons to the 1937 questionnaire can be made with those from 1928 and 1947.

1928

Ronald Colman	Dolores del Rio
Richard Dix	Betty Balfour
Douglas Fairbanks Snr	Clara Bow
Adolphe Menjou	Esther Ralston
Syd Chaplin	Vilma Banky
Charlie Chaplin	Florence Vidor

1947

James Mason	Margaret Lockwood
Stewart Grainger	Ingrid Bergman
Ray Milland	Bette Davis
Alan Ladd	Phyllis Calvert
Bing Crosby	Greer Garson
John Mills	Patricia Roc
Laurence Olivier	Vivien Leigh
Humphrey Bogart	Jeanne Crain
Spencer Tracy	Joan Fontaine
Gary Cooper	Dorothy McGuire

West End Kinema

Situated at the top of Silksworth Row Bank where once stood Ye Old Coffee House, the West End opened on 12th December 1912. Nicknamed the 'Top House' it never went over to talking pictures and closed down in 1929.

WEST END CINEMA

JUST AT THE TOP OF SILKSWORTH ROW.
RICHARDSON'S PICTURES.
Monday to Wednesday :—Two-Part Drama, "THE COMEDIAN'S MASH," Picture of Stage Life. "In god we Trust," Xmas Drama, and other subjects.
CHRISTMAS DAY AT THE CINEMA—Special Performances at 6.30 and 8.30.
GRAND MATINEE ON BOXING DAY at 2.30
Entire Change of Programme,
Usual Times and Prices

Above: The programme for Christmas 1913.

The site of the West End Kinema today. The picture hall would have stood on the central reservation of Silksworth Row just before the roundabout (where the large lamp post now stands).

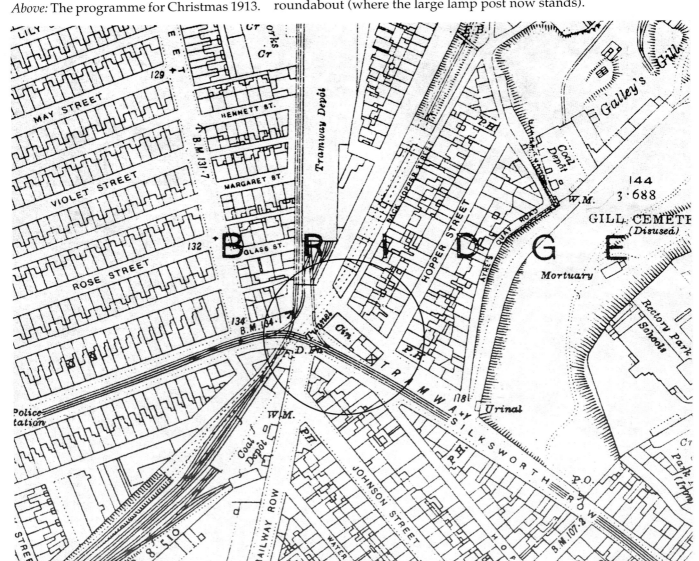

The West End Kinema can be seen on this map of the Bridge Ward from 1919.

Picture House

Whenever the Picture House crops up in conversation on the subject of Sunderland's cinema history, it is one of the best remembered, and those who are old enough to recall going there always call it by its nickname 'The Ranch'. Situated in High Street West, it was opened on 16th December 1912. The first film shown was the drama *His Mother's Picture* and the music was provided by the Viennese Orchestra. An unusual feature of the cinema was its sliding roof/ceiling which was meant to open in hot weather.

In later years never a week went by when there was not a western ... or as they called them in those days 'cowboy picture' screened, and as a result of this it was given the nickname 'The Ranch'. *Below:* A typical western programme on the Picture House.

One morning in 1926 a long queue formed outside the Picture House, a young William Douglass joined the line of men, not to see the film, but to apply for the vacancy of junior projectionist. Young William got the job, one which demanded a great amount of skill. When the electrical equipment broke down, the projector had to be operated by hand, keeping a steady speed during the emergency. At the time talkies were introduced at the Picture House one of the early successes was the musical *Blossom Time*, which played to packed houses for four or five weeks. In 1935 Mr. Douglas moved to the new Black's Regal in South Shields and after six months as chief projectionist was promoted to chief engineer and stage manager. In 1940 he joined Kalee Ltd. as a representative for four northern counties. At the end of the war he returned to Kalee for a year before joining the Royal Air Force Cinema Corporation, first as cinema manager then as area supervisor.

On his return to Sunderland he re-joined Black's as a

The Picture House during its final week.

relief manager at Byker, and in 1950 as manager of the Royal in Bedford Street. In 1958 he became circuit supervisor, but the following year Black's cinemas were taken over by Rank who offered him his old job back at the Royal.

The Royal became a Top Rank bingo club in 1964 and William Douglass stayed there till his retirement in 1970.

The Picture House closed down on 30th September 1966 with *Our Man Flint*, and demolished shortly afterwards to make way for the shopping complex which includes the entrance to the Bridges in High Street West. It has the distinction of being the longest lasting cinema in the town ... 54 years (as opposed to the Ritz which ceased to be classed as a cinema in 1974, from then on being regarded as a multi-screen complex).

Savoy

The Savoy at Southwick was opened by a F.W. de Lentman on 16th December 1912, but shortly afterwards came under the control of the Oliver family which had its origins in the Newcastle area. Management of this family run cinema was made up of George, former mining engineer, his wife Maude, George Jnr., and daughter Joyce.

The projectionist for many years was Alf Marshall, brother of Maude and one of four brothers who ran cinemas in the Forest Hall, and Whitley Bay areas, as well as the Bromarsh in Sunderland. The Marshall family had built up their cinema interests by way of Bioscope exhibitions in fairgrounds around the north.

George Oliver Snr. passed on shortly before the outbreak of the Second World War, and control of the Savoy was left to his son. Young 'Georgie' however was conscripted into the Army, and during his absence on active service in the Middle East the cinema was run by Mrs. Oliver assisted by Joyce, till the end of the hostilities.

They ran a two house system as to the more popular continuous programme, and became well known for its late finishing. On occasions patrons from outside the Southwick area would leave before the end of the 'big picture' in order to catch the last tram home.

Towards the end of the war the Savoy introduced live variety shows on Sunday evenings but due to a lack of interest was scrapped and it went back to pictures.

Something quite unique about the Savoy was the fact that, unlike any other picture hall in Sunderland, it projected the films from behind the screen.

In line with the decline of the fifties, the Savoy closed down on 7th March 1959 with Gregory Peck in *The Man in the Grey Flannel Suit*. The building is now used as a Bingo Hall.

Above: The Savoy in 1912.

Below: Plans showing the Savoy before alterations in 1930.

Alf Marshall,
projectionist at the Savoy, younger brother of Will one time owner of the Bromarsh.

Above: Plans for alterations to the Savoy in 1930.

Right: The Savoy Bingo hall today. The Savoy was one of three Sunderland picture houses to close in 1959.

Silent Music

In the days before talkies distributors would send out musical suggestions to be played during films. *Right:* Suggestions sent to cinemas for the film *Marked Money*.

Synopsis and musical score of film would have to be rehearsed by either pianist or small orchestra (which ever the cinema could afford) before opening night.

Sound effects such as horses galloping, bells ringing, thunder etc, would be performed in conjunction with score by people behind the screen.

Marked Money was released in 1929 just as the talkies were first being produced. The review in *Variety* described *Marked Money* as the "mildest sort of romantic comedy that will just about make the grade in the grinds as the lesser portion of a double bill ... Titles of the obvious variety don't help this flicker a bit."

When the film was shown at the Millfield Kinema the *Echo* said *Marked Money* provided "excellent entertainment in silent films." Also on the bill were two comedies and the Gazette.

MUSICAL SUGGESTIONS

to

"MARKED MONEY"

By ROY ROBERTSON

Mono
MAR 24-1930

	Titles and Action Cues	Music Suggested	Style of Music	Composer	Publisher
1	At screening ...	The Song of the Sea	Ballad Fox Trot...	Kunneke	Feldman
2	At ship in dock at anchor	Calm...	Misterioso	Kay	Foster
3	At boy with monkey (interior)	Spangles	Light Int.	Bratton	Witmark
4	It's account of murder ...	Grave and Largamente	Drama Broad ...	Sibelius	Lafleur
5	You ain't leaving me alone	In Love	Sentimental Andante	Howgill	Hawkes
6	At crook telephoning ...	Agitato Misterioso	Misterioso	Delmas-Popy	Liber
7	As man snatches bag ...	Storm at Sea and Danger	Agitato Heavy ...	Leuschner	Liber
8	As Cook is seen coming downstairs ...	Heave Ho	Nautical Allegro ...	Copping	Berlin, N.Y.
9	As Captain reads letter ...	Farewell	Andante Romantic	Howgill	Hawkes
10	As niece and boy arrive at door	The Love Dance	Light Entr'acte ...	Hoschna	Feldman
11	Boy and Captain with money box	Shiver M'Timbers	Nautical Allegro ...	Elliot-Smith	Boosey
12	At niece on stairs ...	Laughing Marionette	Light Entr'acte ...	Collins	Boosey
13	If the captain ...	Leaving Port ...	Nautical Allegro ...	Howgill	Hawkes
14	At C.U. of serpent on cook's body	Sailors Don't Care	Nautical Two Step	Rudd	Feldman
15	At boy at door with car ...	The River girl ...	Intermezzo	Engleman	Bosworth
16	Mess in more ways than one	Overture Bouffe ...	Light Comedy Overture	Curzon	Dix
17	As medallion falls into soup	1st six bars of Lost Happiness	Misterioso Dramatico	Dyck	Liber
18	Segue ...	Jealousy	Appassionato	Engleman	Bosworth
19	At C.U. of alarm clock ...	The Hobbledehoy	Comedy Misterioso	Olsen	Hawkes
20	As cook takes money box down	Fun on deck in 8	A La Misterioso in 8	Howgill	Hawkes
21	As boy comes downstairs...	Misterioso No. 36	Tense Misterioso	Brockton	Boosey
22	At attack on girl ...	Hurry No. 1 ...	Agitato ...	Lake	Boosey
23	As lover arrives in car ...	Misterious Stranger	Misterioso	Kay	F. & Day
24	As cook attacks boy ...	Desperation	Appassionato	Schad	Lafleur
25	At crooks in car ...	Hurry No. 20 ...	Agitato	Engleman	Bosworth
26	At telephone ringing ...	Astir ...	Agitato	Berge	F. & Day
27	Break at smash with milk cart. Segue	Fight Agitato ...	Agitato	Engleman	Bosworth
28	As lover and boy arrive in car	Agitato Misterioso	Misterioso	Curzon	Dix
29	At attack on crook	Sous Les Tenailles	Agitato	Fosse	Yves, Paris
30	As aeroplane starts	Storm scene	Agitato	Engleman	Bosworth
31	As aeroplane lands	Extase from last Tempo Primo	Flowing Happy ...	Daras	Daras
32	At C.U. of boy with wedding notice ...	The Wedding Glide	Comedy Wedding One Step	Horsch	Feldman

CUE TO FINISH PICTURE WHEN HAT IS CHASED.

Gem

Southwick's other cinema, the Gem in Clockwell Street, was opened on 1st July 1913 by James H. Noble of the well known local fairground family. Converted from a small chapel with seating for about three hundred, it was certainly Sunderland's smallest cinema. Mr. Noble also had the distinction of having opened the town's first radio shop which was in Green Street.

The Gem did not get off to a good start as the first film booked ... *The Devil's Daughter* was late arriving and as a consequence the first night audience had to endure a long delay before the show commenced. As one of the first proper picture houses it had a comparatively short life, closing down in 1924 on the premature death of Jimmy Noble. The building later became the premises of the local National Assistance Board.

A wintery scene of Southwick Council workmen mending the road in front of the Gem. The Gem was housed in the Workmen's Institute on the corner of Clockwell Street and Mary Street.

Millfield Kinema

One of the classics of the silent screen *Antony & Cleopatra* (Vitagraph 1908) opened up the Millfield in Hylton Road on 24th November 1913. It was known by its nickname the 'Milly'.

One of the earliest sound on disc films *My Old Dutch* (an Albert Chevalier song) was shown there in 1916, it starred Albert Chevalier himself and Florence Turner the famous Vitagraph girl. When talkies were introduced in 1929, Kalee 8 projectors and the B.T.H. sound systems were installed. In the immediate post war years Ted Dobson was the chief operator, and 'Lamby' the chucker out kept everyone in order. Ted Prior was the manager when the Milly closed down on 20th September 1959 with *The Sheep Man* starring Glenn Ford.

Below: The *Sunderland Echo* report on the Milly shortly before its opening.

The Millfield Kinema building today.

The "Millfield Picture House," which opens on Monday first, has been erected to meet the demand for a good place of entertainment in the West End of town.

It is a complete theatre—the stage being fitted to accommodate either sketches or turns, which are to alternate with picture subjects; these are to be a speciality of this theatre, and to ensure a good, bright and steady picture no expense has been spared to procure the very latest projectors and electric fittings to bring about this result. The operators' room and rewinding room are spacious and exceptionally well ventilated, and are planned to secure a quick service of films.

The auditorium is fitted throughout with upholstered tip-up chairs, ensuring a comfortable seat to every member of the audience.

The theatre will be run on the popular "two houses a night" principle, and as the management have all the means at hand to produce the best of pictures and to accommodate the most elaborate sketches, there is no doubt it will be a favourite place of resort for the inhabitants of the West End in search of up-to-date entertainment.

The theatre is situated immediately adjoining the Millfield Station, and the electric cars pass the door every few minutes. The seating capacity is about 1,500. Mr John Harley, late lecturer at the Palace, has been appointed manager and lecturer. He says his motto is "Always the latest—only the best,"

Gaiety

The Gaiety at the bottom of High Street East opened shortly before Christmas 1913 and there are probably more uncomplimentary remarks made about this cinema than any other local hall. Nobody outside the East End would ever admit to having been there, yet it is still the source of many happy recollections amongst present and former residents of the area who are old enough to remember those days when it was packed to capacity almost every night.

The first film show given was headed by *Thy Will Be Done* and at the outbreak of the First World War that classic melodrama *Maria Marten – Murder in the Red Barn* was screened. In 1921 The East End Picture Palace Company took control with Percy Pawson as manager, and during the thirties talent competitions were held with prizes of groceries offered to the contestants. The Gaiety's first talking picture, *Dancing Dynamite* with George Raft in the starring role was shown in 1932, and shortly after that Billy Bolam, the best remembered name associated with the cinema was installed as manager.

It is often said that in the days of the depression you could gain entrance to the Gaiety on the presentation of a jam at the pay-box. A half pound jar was worth a halfpenny and a pound jar a penny. There were cinemas during that time which did allow this kind of bartering system. There is absolutely no truth however in the story of the couple who went to the Gaiety one evening, produced a ten shilling note ... and got jam-jars for change! One such story, however, is absolutely true. In the mid-thirties a local shipyard worker once took into

The Gaiety.

work a new roll of admission tickets for the Gaiety, which he sold for a third of the price each to his workmates. The following evening the local press in its review of the town's film shows reported that, "the Gaiety played to a full house - but only 9d was taken at the pay-box!"

The East End lost its only remaining cinema in March 1958 when the Gaiety was demolished to make way for a block of multi-storey flats.

Christine Norden

Sunderland born actress, and sex symbol of the forties, Christine was born in Sunderland Maternity Home on 28th December 1924. Christened Christine Mary Lydia Thornton, she spent her early life at 381 Hylton Road, and worked at Steel's and Books Fashions. Made her screen debut in *Night Beat* (1947). Other films include, *Mine Own Executioner*, *Reluctant Heroes*, *A Case for P.C. 49*, *An Ideal Husband*, *Lady Windemere's Fan* and *Saints and Sinners*.

She left England to live in America in 1952 and in 1960 became a U.S. citizen. Starring in several Broadway productions, and in 1967 created a sensation when appearing topless in the musical *Tenderloin*. In 1978 returned to England for good. Sunderland's most famous female film star died in 1988.

Right: Christine Norden and Kieron Moore in a scene from *Saints and Sinners*.

Queen's Hall Kinema

The opening of the Queen's Hall Kinema in December 1912 brought the number of moving picture venues in the town up to twenty, just one below the all-time peak which was to be reached three year later with the opening of the Roker in Roker Avenue.

This small but luxurious cinema, situated between the clock tower at Mackie's Corner and the old Grand Hotel in Bridge Street certainly went out of its way to attract customers. With so much competition around, exhibitors would offer all kinds of extras, and the Queen's Hall Kinema was no exception. Tea was offered free of charge to patrons in the balcony, a Bijou Orchestra would be in attendance, and there was also a mini Evening News edited by the manager, and anyone having a signed copy would be admitted free of charge to the grand stalls.

The box-office staff wore long ankle length skirts and blouses with large collars over the shoulders and tiny bib aprons. Commissionaires and pageboys had the usual braid and buttons, and the manager would always be seen in full tails evening dress.

An idea of the fare provided may be gauged from a programme which reads:

"Queen's Hall Kinema, Sunderland open 2-30 till 10-30 pm. Today's programme includes:
Are We Ready, *The Breast of the Tide*, *The Cry of the Captive*,

A ticket for the Queen's Hall Kinema.

Fatty Joins the Forces, *Kum & Laugh & Scream*, *Gaumont Graphic*. Programme changed twice weekly."

Prices of admission were Stalls 9d and 6d, Front stalls 3d, Balcony 1/-.

Like the Theatre de Luxe in Fawcett Street, the Queen's closed down in 1917 in face of overwhelming opposition from the newly opened Havelock, which stood only fifty yards away at Mackie's corner.

The Queen's Hall Kinema before the First World War.

Havelock
(Gaumont)

Provincial Cinematograph Theatres opened the Havelock on 16th December 1915, on the site where once stood the Havelock House which in 1898 had been destroyed in the town's biggest ever fire. Its first programme of films was *The Girl Who Might Have Been*, *The Night Before Christmas*, *Climbing The Jung Frau* and *The Haunted Hat*, with accompaniment by a ten piece orchestra. The orchestra would become redundant on the installation of a two manual Wurlitzer organ in 1926.

The Havelock's main claim to fame is that it introduced talking pictures to Sunderland in 1929 with Al Jolson in *The Singing Fool*. It ran from 15th July to the 10th August and attracted an audience of 120,000!

A splendid cinema for its time, it forced some of the lesser competition out of business almost immediately. It could seat 1700 in the circle and stalls, was run by an all male staff, of which the page boys in their blue uniforms and pill-box hats were a feature, and was the only local cinema which provided deaf aids, attached to the end

The Havelock on Mackie's Corner, the busy junction of Fawcett Street and High Street West.

A Havelock cinematograph machine between the wars.

seats for local people. Provincial Cinematograph Theatres was taken over by Gaumont British in the 1960s, and the Havelock was re-named the Gaumont. The Gaumont was eventually taken over by Rank, but no further name change took place till it finally closed down on 15th June 1963 with the British film *Taste Of Fear*.

Christmas at the Havelock

The *Sunderland Echo* on Christmas Eve 1929 noted how the Havelock staff put on their own festive entertainment:

An enterprising Christmas feature is the brief Dickensian sketch very ably acted with Mr Don Hartness as Scrooge, Mr Rushworth (manager of the theatre) as Marley's Ghost and a page boy, Master Jack Walker. This novel item elicited warm appreciation, also the Christmas carols by the Havelock cafe and theatre staff.

THE HAVELOCK.

Is "SILENT" NO LONGER.

To-day—

See & Hear

AL JOLSON

IN

The Singing Fool

100 TALKING, SINGING, AND SOUND.

AT

1-10, 3-5, 5-0, 6-55, and 8-50.

The Best Times to come are at 1-0 and 8-50.

HAVE LUNCH IN THE HAVELOCK CAFE.

Above: Sunderland's first talkie at the Havelock.

Right: Al Jolson in a scene from *The Singing Fool.*

The splendid interior of the Havelock.

Roker Variety Theatre

Under the same management as the Villiers, the Roker Variety Theatre in Roker Avenue opened its doors for business on 15th October 1915. The date of opening is significant as all public building was curtailed at the outbreak of the First World War, and the Roker along with the Havelock had to apply for permission to complete construction of the buildings. Ownership of the Roker and Villiers (Sunderland Amusements Ltd.) was shared by local businessmen George Clark, Charles Oliver, Tom Murray, Bill Robertson, Harry Randall and Tommy Johnson.

The Roker was the first Sunderland Cinema to draw on ordinary electricity in the late 1920s after using a special supply of direct current. However, even this technological marvel did not prevent the occasional breakdown, then the film would have to be hand cranked through the projector.

Special mention has been made in this work of certain individuals who in their own special way, represent all those dedicated people who worked in the cinema business, and contributed greatly to the enjoyment it gave to all cinemagoers over the last century.

One such person was the late Arthur Ratcliffe, who began work at the Roker as a 'lime boy' in 1916, and gradually worked his way up to the position of Chief Projectionist, which he held till the cinema's closure in 1961. It was Arthur in fact who supplied me with most of the background information concerning the early days of the cinema in Sunderland.

The attributes required of a good operator are a complete dedication to a job which called on you to work very unsociable hours, a very alert mind, quick reflexes and self control in any number of unexpected emergencies. The Roker had in Arthur Ratcliffe an operator who had

Roker Variety Theatre.

all these qualities. During a career which spanned 45 years he witnessed all the phases in the technical development and presentation of the motion picture. As a lime boy one of his early tasks had been to operate the spotlight for the variety acts, and help in the carrying of films between the Roker and its twin cinema the Villiers. He saw the modernization of the Roker which came with the conversion to sound in 1931, and the new challenge the medium brought.

At any time ... without warning ... a chief may have to deal with any one of a number of emergencies ... the film catching fire ... a snap ... a breakdown in equipment ... or the failure of the advertised film to arrive on time. How quickly he reacts in situations like this, with a restless audience 'out front' can make or break an operator. That is when he needs the quick reflexes and self control in an emergency. I have seen Arthur survive many such situations, with the audience quite unaware of the real life drama taking place behind the scenes.

When the silent films were shown the chief had to spend one morning a week rehearsing each new film with the ten piece orchestra. He recalled, "They used to send a synopsis of the film and a music score, but we always had a run-through with the orchestra, to ensure they played the right music at the right time."

Friday nights during the twenties were trial nights when local amateurs had the chance on the stage between pictures. These nights were so popular that mounted police had to be called in, to control the queues that thronged the pavement right up to the Wheat Sheaf. The Friday cine-variety nights were also very popular during the Second World War.

The Roker's organ was a two manual, 16 ranks 'straight', built by the Sunderland firm of William Sewell, and when no longer required it was dismantled, some pipework being installed in St. Andrew's Church, Chippenham and the remainder scrapped.

In 1930 the projection room was moved from the rear stalls to the back of the circle area and the following year their first talkie *Sally* starring Marylin Miller and Joyce Brown was shown.

Closure came on 8th April 1961 with the Disney film *Darby O'Gill and the Little People.* Arthur Ratcliffe told a *Sunderland Echo* reporter at the time, "It nearly broke my heart when the Roker closed. I had helped to entertain thousands of Sunderland people over the years and I really enjoyed every minute of it." Arthur died in 1973 after a long illness.

Above: An advert from the *Echo* of 25th March 1930. The Sharkey v Scott fight was one of those films that had to be transported back and forth between the Villiers.

King's Theatre

Before we go on to talk about the King's, which was opened in 1906, it would be interesting to pause and look at some local buildings which were either under construction or opened that year.

New offices of Sunderland and South Shields Water Company were being erected on the corner of John Street and Borough Road and the Orchard Cottage at the junction of Tatham Street and Borough Road had been demolished to make way for the Board of Trade offices. Construction of the new Police Station and the nearby Fire Station was well under way. Extensions to the Thompson Memorial Hall in Dundas Street were being carried out, and the new Baths and Wash-houses in Hendon Road were completed and opened on 28th May. St. Joseph's Roman Catholic Church at Millfield, and St. Patrick's School in Walton Lane both opened that year, while the magnificent St. Andrew's Church at Roker was nearing completion. Pride of place however (for the purpose of this book) must go to the King's Theatre in Crowtree Road, which opened on 24th December that year, only seven months after building had begun and seven months ahead of the Empire Theatre. This most beautiful of theatres which stood within a hundred yards of the Palace, Avenue and Empire, added a whole new meaning to theatre luxury.

The King's Theatre in its heyday.

KING'S THEATRE.

Managing Directors - Mr. ERNEST STEVENS & MR. R. C. BUCHANAN.
Resident Manager - - - - MR. HARRY L. CARLO.

TELEPHONE 1008.

This Charming Up-to-Date Theatre Opened December 24th, 1906,

With Grand Christmas Pantomime,

Little Red Riding Hood,

BY STANLEY ROGERS,

Is one of the most commodious in the North of England. Built from Designs of Mr. William Hope by Messrs. Davidson, of Newcastle. Lighted throughout by Electricity. Ventilated and Heated on the latest scientific principles. Seating Capacity, 2,300.

This Theatre will be booked in conjunction with the King's Theatre, Edinbro', Grand Theatre, Glasgow, and Scotland's Provincial Theatres, therefore, commanding Companies hitherto unobtainable in Sunderland.

Seats can be booked from 2/6 upwards at Messrs. Ferry and Foster's, 3, Bridge Street. No extra fee. Telephone 77.

PRICES OF ADMISSION: Private Boxes to hold 5 Persons, £1 11s. 6d. Orchestra Stalls, 3s.; Stalls 1s. 6d.; Dress Circle, 2s.; Balcony Stalls (Tip-up chairs 1s.); Gallery, 6d. Early Door 6d. Extra; Gallery, 3d. Children Half-Price to all Matinees and Evening performances, except on Holidays.

The Premier Theatre of Sunderland.

In 1906 money was being poured into the theatre and music hall, for it was believed that this was where the future of the entertainment industry lay. All five local theatres, however, including the Royal in Bedford Street, would eventually become dependent on moving pictures for their life blood. In the case of the Empire it would be an intermittent flirtation which it would finally cast off to become the foremost variety theatre in the North of England. In the midst of all the justifiable praise heaped on the Empire, one must not forget the King's, which opened before its more illustrious neighbour and was just as popular among local cinema and theatregoers alike.

Many new features hitherto untried in theatrical building were introduced into the construction of the King's. The most revolutionary of these was the cantilever principle to support the circle and gallery areas. Anyone who went to the Palace and was unlucky enough to be seated behind one of the supporting pillars will realise the merits of the cantilever principle. Another interesting feature was the use for the first time of Hennebique Ferro Concrete in the construction of the circle and gallery, making the theatre virtually fireproof. Seating too was arranged to a different plan, there being no pit area, this traditional part of the theatre becoming what we now know as the stalls. Replacing the pit were the balcony stalls, with comfortable tip-up seats at a shilling a time.

Managing directors of the new theatre were Ernest Stevens and Robbie Buchanan, two Scots who also controlled sixteen other theatres in Scotland and the provinces. First resident manager was Harry L. Carlo one time manager of the Palace theatre.

The two Scots timed it to perfection when they opened the King's for business on Christmas Eve 1906 with the pantomime *Little Red Riding Hood*. The first presentation of moving pictures came in 1913, and on 22nd February 1915 the first Kinemacolour films were shown. The Blacks took over in 1918, but shortly afterwards sold their interest in the theatre.

The King's first talkie was *Behind The Curtain* starring Warner Baxter, screened on 6th January 1930.

A Vincent 3 manual, 26 ranks 'straight organ with tubular pneumatic action was installed in 1918 and opened by David Clegg. It was rebuilt in 1928 by William Sewell as a three manual, 29 rank organ divided either side of the proscenium arch. The organ was destroyed along with the theatre by enemy action.

During the Second World War, Sunday evening concerts at the King's, with resident orchestras led by Al Flush and Peter Fielding were very popular. (Al Flush

and his orchestra were resident at the Rink Ballroom for many years).

The end of this wonderful cinema/theatre came on 16th May 1943 when it was destroyed by enemy bombing. The last films were *Rookies* starring Abbot & Costello and *When Johnny Comes Marching Home*.

The charred remains of the King's.

Victory

Formerly the Smyrna Chapel and then taken over by Sunderland Nursing Institute, the Victory at the junction of Borough Road and Smyrna Place was opened by Victory Cinemas in 1920.

Along with the Gaiety in High Street it catered for residents of the East End of the town. Talent nights with food parcels as prizes were very popular during the depression years, and Jimmy Cagney was a firm favourite with patrons

Mr. George Lamb was manager here for a long time, but his reign came to an abrupt end on 15th April 1941 when the Victory (along with Victoria Hall) was destroyed by enemy bombing. A typical Victory film *Gangs of Chicago* starring Barton McLane and Lloyd Nolan was the last film shown.

Smyrna Chapel

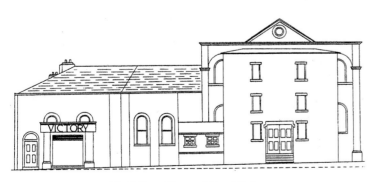
Building Plan of the Victory.

A footnote to the Victory's destruction appeared in the *Sunderland Echo* after the raid:

End of the Show

Men engaged in "clearing up the mess" in a North-East Coast town* which recently suffered a heavy attack from the air came across the only remains of the reels of film which had been showing at a wrecked cinema the previous night.

It was eight inches of film showing the King's portrait surrounded by the emblems of Empire: and of course, the only time this film is seen is at the end of the show.

*Sunderland was not named due to wartime censorship.

Wartime

At the outbreak of the Second World War all cinemas were ordered to close as it was considered risky in the event of an air raid to have large numbers of people under one roof. They remained closed for a fortnight, re-opening on 18th September after a government re-think. It was decided that their contribution to the morale of the people outweighed by far the risk of cinemas and other such forms of entertainment being destroyed while shows were in progress. As far as Sunderland was concerned this conclusion proved to be absolutely right. During the war years there were a total of 17 cinemas (and the Empire) in operation. Out of this number we lost the Bromarsh (1943), King's (1943), Victory (1941) and the Victoria Hall (1941), all destroyed during the night when empty without any loss of life. In the book *Picture Pioneers* by G.J. Mellor the author says that the Bromarsh was "bombed during a performance, and many people were killed." This is not true, however during the air raid which destroyed the Bromarsh, several were killed in a nearby communal air raid shelter.

Pictures scheduled for showing on some of the town's cinemas at the outbreak of war were:

The Ritz	*Midnight* with Don Ameche
Havelock	*The Mikado* with Kenny Baker
King's	*Newsboys Home* with Jackie Cooper
Marina	*Luck of the Navy* with Jack Oakie
Millfield	*Maytime* with Nelson Eddy & Jeanette Macdonald
Palace	*Trouble Brewing* with George Formby
Picture House	*Algiers* with George Boyer
Plaza	*Huckleberry Finn* with Mickey Rooney
Regal	*Stagecoach* with John Wayne
Regent	*They Drive By Night* with Emlyn Williams
Roker & Villiers	*My Irish Molly* with Binkie Stuart

During the war cinemas enjoyed their biggest audiences ever, as crowds flocked to them escaping the grim realities of everyday life. However in the immediate post-war years audiences began to decline. Not only had peoples attitudes changed, the cinemas were no longer the glittering dream palaces which they had been at the outbreak of hostilities. Television, gradually growing ever more popular, was given a great boost with the transmission of the Coronation in June 1953, and again in 1955 with the introduction of Independent Television. Beginning with the Palace in 1956, Sunderland lost a total of six halls in the fifties, and a further seven in the sixties. Leaving only the Regal (Odeon) and the Ritz open, in a town that over the years can boast to having had a total of thirty two cinemas and other venues for moving pictures.

The best of the War Years films.

Arsenic and Old Lace	Clark Gable
Blood and Sand	Tyrone Power Linda Darnell
Boom Town	Clark Gable Spencer Tracy
Citizen Kane	Orson Welles Joseph Cotton
Dr Jekyll & Mr Hyde	Spencer Tracy Ingrid Bergman
Fanny by Gaslight	James Mason Phyllis Calvert
For Whom The Bells Toll	Gary Cooper Ingrid Bergman
Gone With the Wind	Clark Gable Vivien Leigh
The Grapes of Wrath	Henry Fonda
Heaven Can Wait	Gene Tierney Don Ameche
Henry V	Laurence Olivier
Its That Man Again	Tommy Handley
Jane Eyre	Orson Welles Joan Fontaine
Kipps	Michael Redgrave
Kitty Foyle	Ginger Rogers
The Little Foxes	Bette Davis Herbert Marshall
The Lost Weekend	Ray Milland
Love on the Dole	Clifford Evans Deborah Kerr
Madame Curie	Greer Garson Walter Pidgeon
Meet me in St Louis	Judy Garland
Now Voyager	Bette Davis Paul Henreid
Pride and Prejudice	Greer Garson Laurence Olivier
Rebecca	Laurence Olivier Joan Fontaine
The Sea Hawk	Errol Flynn
Sergeant York	Gary Cooper Joan Leslie
Ox Bow Incident	Henry Fonda Dana Andrews
This Happy Breed	Robert Newton Celia Johnson
Waterloo Bridge	Robert Taylor Vivien Leigh
The Wizard of Oz	Judy Garland

Some of the films that made us laugh and forget the War ...

Andy Hardy's Double Life	Mickey Rooney
Banana Ridge	Robertson Hare Alfred Drayton
Band Waggon	Arthur Askey
Broadway Melody of 1940	Fred Astaire
Duffy's Tavern	Betty Hutton
The Fleet's In	Betty Hutton William Holden
Garrison Follies	Barry Lupino
The Ghost Train	Arthur Askey Richard Murdoch
The Great Dictator	Charlie Chaplin
Great Guns	Laurel & Hardy
Hellzapoppin	Olsen & Johnson
Hi Gang	Bebe Daniels Ben Lyon
Incendiary Blonde	Betty Hutton
Laugh It Off	Tommy Trinder
Let George Do It	George Formby
Love Crazy	William Powell
One Night in the Tropics	Abbot & Costello
Pack Up your Troubles	Wylie Watson
Saps at Sea	Laurel & Hardy
Sing As We Go	Gracie Fields
Somewhere in England	Frank Randle
Spare A Copper	George Formby
Women Aren't Angels	Robertson Hare Alfred Drayton

Regal
(Odeon)

Built on the site once occupied by the Olympia Pleasuredrome in Holmeside, Black's Regal was the biggest and certainly the most luxurious cinema in Sunderland's history. The architects were Gray & Evans and the construction was carried out by local builders A.J. Rankin, who completed the building, which cost £100,000 in a year. It boasted the most up to date projection equipment, could seat 2,500, and had a staff of more than sixty.

Prices of admission on opening were: Royal Circle 2/-, Dress Circle 1/6-, Circle 1/4. Stalls 1/- and Front Stalls 7d, with reduced prices on Saturday's and holidays.

The directorate of the new cinema were Alfred & Edward Black (managing directors), Roland Jennings M.P. (chairman), Ronald Sutcliffe and George F. Hill.

On opening day, Easter Monday, 28th March 1932, a crowd gathered for the opening ceremony performed by the Mayor, Alderman E.H. Brown. The first programme featured Laurel & Hardy in *One Good Turn*, the Paramount News and *Fisherman's Paradise* described as a unique item of interest. The main feature was *Out of the Blue* with Gene Garrard and Jessie Matthews. On stage was the Myron Pearl Company in *Viennese Echoes* with Hugh Ormond the English tenor, accompanied by the Regal Orchestra conducted by Arnold Eagle (Eagle of the Regal).

The old Regal building today is run as a Bingo hall.

Jessie Matthews in *Out of the Blue*, the first film to be shown at the Regal.

The Regal continued to present extravagant stage shows until about 1945, and wartime Sunday concerts were very popular with Wearsiders.

The Regal's mighty 3 manual, 9 ranks Compton organ is thought to have been designed by Arnold Eagle, the cinema's opening organist. In common with other cinema organs of the period the illuminating console was on a lift. 'Eagle of the Regal' began his long career at the Victoria Hall and became musical director for the Black's Scala Cinema in South Shields at the age of twenty. He moved to the south of England, but returned in 1932 to take over at the new Regal. In 1946 he became conductor of the Empire Theatre Orchestra until his retirement. He passed away in 1966 at the age of 64.

In 1959 the Black's circuit was taken over by the Rank Organisation and the Regal became the Odeon. Seating capacity about this time was cut by 300 and the front stalls entrance in Park Lane was closed permanently in 1964.

The Odeon closed down on 8th February 1975 for conversion to three screens, the last film being *The Man With The Golden Gun* starring Roger Moore. It re-opened

Black's Regal Theatre in the late 1930s.

as the Odeon Film Centre on 9th March 1975 with *The Taking of Pelham 1.2.3.* on Screen One, *The Mad Adventures of Rabbi Jacob* on Screen Two and *The Odessa File* on Screen Three. Only a few years later the popular manager Ray Cook, winner of the film exhibitors' star award on more than one occasion passed away on 26th April 1979.

During 1981 the future closure was announced with plans for the Odeon to become a Bingo hall. However before closure took place a special 50th Anniversary concert was held on Sunday 28th March 1982, featuring Phil Kelsall, organist at The Tower Ballroom, Blackpool. Closure took place three months later on 26th June. The last films shown were *One Flew Over The Cuckoo's Nest* on Screen One, *Star Wars* and *The Empire Strikes Back* on Screen Two, and *Mary Millington's True Blue Confessions* on Screen Three. Brett Childs, manager on closure is now manager of the Empire's Studio cinema.

Manager Brett Childs *(right)* and projectionist Bill Souter on the last day of the Odeon as a cinema.

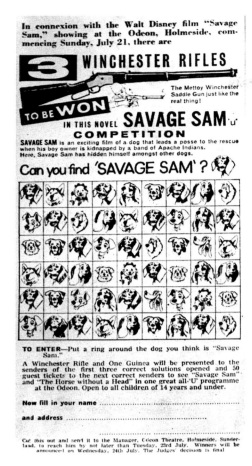

In connexion with the Walt Disney film "Savage Sam," showing at the Odeon, Holmeside, commencing Sunday, July 21, there are

3 WINCHESTER RIFLES

The Mettoy Winchester Saddle Gun just like the real thing!

TO BE WON

IN THIS NOVEL SAVAGE SAM 'u'
COMPETITION

SAVAGE SAM is an exciting film of a dog that leads a posse to the rescue when his boy owner is kidnapped by a band of Apache Indians. Here, Savage Sam has hidden himself amongst other dogs.

Can you find 'SAVAGE SAM'?

TO ENTER—Put a ring around the dog you think is "Savage Sam."

A Winchester Rifle and One Guinea will be presented to the senders of the first three correct solutions opened and 50 guest tickets to the next correct senders to see "Savage Sam" and "The Horse without a Head" in one great all-'U' programme at the Odeon. Open to all children of 14 years and under.

Now fill in your name ....

and address ....

Cut this out and send it to the Manager, Odeon Theatre, Holmeside, Sunderland, to reach him by not later than Tuesday, 23rd July. Winners will be announced on Wednesday, 24th July. The Judges' decision is final

Children's Time

Left: A competition run in conjunction with the *Sunderland Echo* offered prizes and tickets to see Walt Disney's *Savage Sam* in July 1963.

Right: The film's appearance at the Odeon was also well advertised in the local press.

A trip to the pictures is often given as a treat to children. In January 1978 members of Witherwack Thistle Club sent their children on one such trip. *Below:* Part of the group of 350 children arrive at the Odeon.

Marina

The thirties saw the building of five new cinemas, and following the Regal came the Marina, the first of the modern suburban halls.

Built by the Hinge Circuit in Sea Road, Fulwell, the residents of Fulwell, even today, some thirty years after it closed, often recall with a great deal of nostalgia, nights spent at the Marina. It was opened to the public on 31st July 1935 by Alderman E.H. Brown, and the first film shown was *Things Are Looking Up* starring Cicely Courtneidge.

The height of its popularity came during the forties and fifties, especially among the younger cinemagoers who would form long queues for the Sunday evening performances, and some may be lucky enough to occupy the double seats provided for courting couples. The Marina closed down on 27th July 1963, with the film *We Joined The Navy* starring Kenneth More. The site is now occupied by a supermarket.

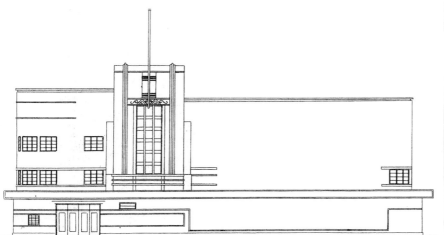
The building plan of the Marina.

Marina staff circ. 1950.

The Marina in Sea Road in 1963.

The foyer of the Marina.

Plaza

The people of Pallion and surrounding districts got their own cinema with the opening of the Plaza in Pallion Road on the evening of the Monday 1st August 1936. The first feature film they saw on that night was *Casino de Paris* starring Al Jolson ... not one of that great film star's best remembered pictures. It was a different story however in the immediate post-war years when *The Jolson Story* with Larry Parks, attracted full houses every night at the Plaza.

When closure came on 12th July 1968 the Plaza had remained open longer than any other suburban cinema in the town. The last film was *Bridge On The River Kwai* with Jack Hawkins and Alec Guinness.

Top right: The Plaza Plan, originally this Pallion cinema was to be called the Rialto, hence the name sign.

Bottom right: The Plaza today, like many of the picture halls that have survived it is now a bingo club..

The Plaza was one of eleven purpose-built cinemas in Sunderland. The others were: Ritz, Havelock, Marina, Millfield Kinema, Regal, Picture House, Regent, Villiers Electric Theatre, Gaiety and Roker.

The Young Ones

There have been many child stars in the history of the cinema, and they were all very popular with Sunderland audiences. The most outstanding ones being: Freddie Bartholomew, Jackie Coogan, Jackie Cooper, the Dead End Kids, Our Gang, Judy Garland, Mickey Rooney, Sabu, Shirley Temple and Jane Withers.

It was Shirley Temple who made the biggest impact of all child stars. Born in 1929 she was first noticed as a possible box-office attraction in the film *Stand Up and Cheer* when she sang *Baby Take a Bow* at the end of the picture. Seven Shirley Temple films were released in 1934, the most popular being: *Now I'll Tell* with Spencer Tracy, *Little Miss Marker*, *Now and Forever* with Gary Cooper and Carole Lombard, and *Bright Eyes* in which she sang her best known song *On the Good Ship Lollipop*, this was the film which gave Jane Withers her big break. *The Little Colonel*, *Our Little Girl*, *Curly Top* and *The Littlest Rebel* came in 1935, making her the number one box office attraction that year, a position she was to hold for the following three years.

The best known of Shirley Temple's pictures, *Rebecca of Sunnybrook Farm* was issued in 1938, and the next year saw her appearing in her first technicolour films ... *The Little Princess* and *Susannah of the Mounties*. Her next technicolour film *The Blue Bird* was the first of her films to lose money, and the next one, *The Young People* was the last for her home studio. In less than three years Shirley Temple had made 24 films, and her earnings reputed to have reached a staggering 3,000,000 dollars. Metro Goldwyn Mayer still had faith in Shirley Temple and in 1941 issued her first comeback film *Kathleen*, followed in 1942 by *Miss Annie Rooney* and *Since You Went Away* in 1943 for which she received a special Academy Award citation. Two more films came in 1945, *The Bachelor and The Bobbysoxer* and *Honeymoon*. These were followed by *The Hagen Girl* in 1947, *Fort Apache* and *Adventure in Baltimore* in 1948, and *Mr. Belvedere Goes to College*, *A Kiss for Corliss* and *The Story of Seabiscuit* all made in 1949.

Jackie Coogan was without doubt the biggest child star of the silent screen. Born in 1914 he was only 18 months old when he appeared in his first movie, *Skinners Boy*. But it was *The Kid* (1920) in which he appeared with Charlie Chaplin that gave him his big break. Praise for his performance came from far and wide and a great future was forecast for the young Coogan, whose acting ability was far in advance of his years. He went on to star in many films including, *Peck's Bad Boy*, *Oliver Twist*, *My Boy* and *Trouble*. Jackie Coogan appeared at the London Palladium in 1928, when his 'Kid' days were over and the star in the descent.

After his comeback film in 1930 Coogan made the gradual fall to playing bit parts on television. In 1964 this one time idol of millions as a lovable child took on the role of Uncle Fester in the TV series, *The Addams Family*, a long way from the little boy with the big cap walking hand in hand with Charlie Chaplin.

Shirley Temple in *Curly Top*.

The child stars gave the filmgoer countless hours of pleasure, and we all had our particular favourite. It may have been Freddie Bartholomew in *David Copperfield* and *Captains Courageous*, The Dead End Kids (Huntz Hall, Bobby Jordan, Billy Halop, Leo Gorcey, Bernard Hunsley and Gabriel Dell) who were given that name after appearing in the film *Dead End* with Humphrey Bogart. The tragic Judy Garland who made her first film in 1936 called *Pigskin Parade* ... which starred another newcomer to the screen Betty Grable. The best remembered film of Judy's is of course *The Wizard of Oz*, still a popular film among children. She co-starred in many films with another great child star of the day ... Mickey Rooney. By the time they began making pictures together Mickey Rooney was already a veteran of more than 100 films. Born in 1920 he made his first appearance on the screen when only three years old, under his real name Joe Yule Jnr. He was chosen from a long list of applicants to play the part of Mickey McGuire in many short films, and in 1932 changed his name to Mickey Rooney. The output of his films in the thirties was fantastic, some of the most popular were: *Manhattan Melodrama*, *Ah Wilderness*, *Midsummer Nights Dream*, *Little Lord Fauntleroy*, *Captains Courageous* and *A Yank at Eton*, all made in 1936. *A Family Affair* (1937) was the forerunner of the successful Andy

Hardy pictures. *Boys Town*, *Huckleberry Finn*, *Young Tom Edison*, *The Human Comedy* and *National Velvet* with Elizabeth Taylor all helped to make Mickey Rooney the number one box office attraction of 1939-40-41.

Mickey Rooney is one of the very few child stars who survived the transitional period between childhood an maturity and remained a star. Looking back on a career spanning more than 70 years and over 600 films, Mickey Rooney can be well pleased with his contribution to our enjoyment of the motion picture.

Above: Children receive presents outside the Havelock after seeing a free show on 30th December 1929. This was an annual event sponsored by the Havelock in memory of the children who perished in the Victoria Hall Disaster of 1883.

Children's Favourites

Top ten children's favourite film stars according to the findings of the Bernstein questionnaire to children in 1947.

Roy Rogers
James Mason
Bing Crosby
Stewart Granger
Margaret Lockwood
Gene Autry
George Formby
Alan Ladd
Tarzan (Johnny Weismuller)

In the days before television children on Wearside, like those all over the country, eagerly looked forward to Saturday matinees. These were special bills for young audiences, consisting of serials, westerns etc. The theme song for these matinees was: "We come along each Saturday morning greeting everybody with a smile."

In the 1930s these used to be held on Saturday afternoons and kids would start queuing early on the morning to get a good seat. At this time youngsters were placed in their seats in an orderly fashion, beginning at the back row down to the front stalls. (Another legacy of the Victoria Hall Disaster.) Those at the end of the queue usually came out with stiff necks.

Pal Palmer recreates the atmosphere of a matinee at the Roker Variety Theatre.

Ritz
(ABC, Cannon)

The two main events of 1937 ... as far as the recreation and leisure activities of Sunderland people were concerned ... were Sunderland's victory over Preston North End in the FA Cup Final, and the opening of the Ritz cinema in Holmeside.

Built on the site of a former cattle market by Union Cinemas, and fitted out most lavishly with chandeliers and deep pile carpets, the Ritz opened on 1st March 1937 with the Astaire and Rogers musical *Swing Time*. Three years later in October 1942 the classic *Gone With the Wind* had its first showing in Sunderland, for a record-breaking six week run.

Union cinemas was taken over by Associated British Cinemas in the early sixties, and the Ritz became the ABC, the name it retained till 1974 when new owners EMI converted it into a two screen complex. The first films screened on the

The Cannon today, one of the last surviving Sunderland cinemas.

new twin cinemas were *Serpico* starring Al Pacino, on Screen One, and *S.P.Y.S.* starring Elliot Gould on Screen Two. Seating capacity before conversion was 1,500, now as the Cannon that figure has been reduced to 762.

The Ritz during its ABC period in the 1970s.

David O. Selznick's blockbuster *Gone With the Wind* was given its world premiere in Atlanta, Georgia in December 1939. Sunderland audiences had to wait another two years and nine months before they had the opportunity to see the multi Oscar-winning film *(below)*.

The Ritz was originally to have been called the Savoy, but there was already one Savoy at Southwick. Union Cinemas always called their new cinemas 'Ritz' anyway, so why they were going to call it the Savoy is one of those strange quirks of cinema history which defy logical explanation.

The *Sunderland Echo* of 8th September 1942 reported:

Ritz Technicolour "Draw" "Gone With The Wind"

"Gone With The Wind" may be the longest film ever screened – its showing at the Ritz Cinema this week takes nearly four hours – but there will be few to complain about this. So brilliantly worked out is this story of civil war-torn America, so much of a unity is the action and so thrilling alive are its main characters that time passes without being noticed. Sunderland has waited long enough to see the film version of Margaret Mitchell's best seller – but it was worth waiting.

The story might well have been written for Clark Gable and Vivien Leigh, who, as Rhett Butler and Scarlet O'Hara, dominate the action. Hollywood's casting, for once, was dead right, and Vivien Leigh's performance as the hard-headed little Southern beauty, who faces disaster and death unshaken in courage, is one which will long be remembered. Leslie Howard and Olivia de Havilland also gives memorable performances.

Technicolour has never been better handled, an the scenes as the refugees stumble out of the blazing town are amazing in their realism. "Gone With The Wind" is something quite out of the ordinary – a film which should not be missed.

Regent

One of the three suburban cinemas opened during the thirties, most cinemagoers who remember and visited them all, would agree the Regent at Grangetown out-shone them all. The spacious and comfortable seating area was all on one level, with a perfect view of the screen from wherever you were seated, and the interior decor was certainly the most beautiful.

It opened to the public on 31st May 1937 with *Rose Marie* starring Nelson Eddy and Jeanette Macdonald, and closed on 3rd June 1961 with *The Big Fisherman* starring Howard Keel.

A supermarket now stands on the site.

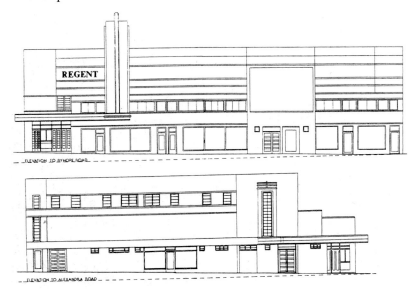

Left: The building plans for the Regent by Architects, J.H. Morton & Son.

Below: The supermarket that was built on the site of the Regent.

The Regent was to remain open for less than a quarter of a century but during that time it was recognised as one of Sunderland's best.

Studios One & Two
(Fairworld)

Above: Studios One & Two, housed in the former Sans Street Mission at the bottom of High Street, and only a hundred yards from where the old Gaiety Cinema stood, was opened by the Star Organisation on 13th January 1969. It began with the David Niven film *The Impossible Years* on Studio One and *A Man and A Woman* on Studio Two. *Below:* A queue winds its way up High Street for a show in the 1970s. In 1976 Studio Two became Studio X, with its film programme self explanatory. Both were re-named in 1977 when taken over by Fairworld *(top right)*. After only four years under their control they relinquished ownership, and the cinema continued for some time as the Eros Cinema Club, showing uncensored films. Unlike all the other cinemas written about in this book, which for more than a century provided family entertainment, the passing into history of the Eros Cinema Club will not be looked on with any regrets.

University of Sunderland

Screen on the River
St. Peter's Campus

TYNESIDE CINEMA

The city's newest cinema lies only a few hundred yards from where Sunderland's first permanent cinema, Monkwearmouth Picture Hall (Bromarsh), once stood. The 400-seat Sir Tom Cowie Theatre at St. Peter's Campus is equipped with state-of-the-art audio visual technology. The University of Sunderland have collaborated with Tyneside Cinema to create a film theatre on the north side of the river for the first time since 1963. Although to begin with the cinema will only be open once a week.

Dr Anne Wright, university vice-chancellor and chief executive, announced that "opening up the university to our local community is a priority and our series of concerts on campus, public lectures and debates have proved very popular. We hope this new facility will encourage even more people to enjoy the superb facilities."

The Launch Preview took place on 14th September 1995 and I was honoured to be asked to 'press the button' at the opening ceremony of Sunderland's latest cinema.

Above: A model of Phase One of St. Peter's Campus. The six-sided building in the centre of the picture is the Sir Tom Cowie Lecture Theatre.

Above: The development under construction sandwiched between the 7th century St. Peter's Church and the River Wear from which the cinema takes its name.

Below: The completed Phase One. St. Peter's Campus will not be totally finished until the early years of the next century.

Index

Black Cat Publications

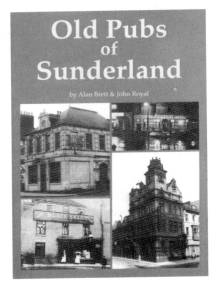

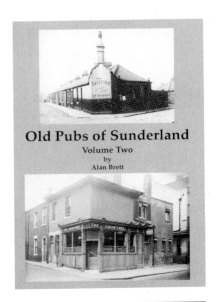

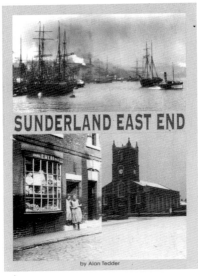

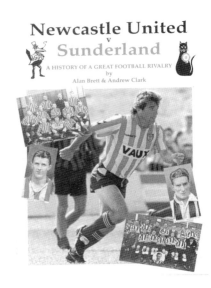